IMAGES
*of America*

# THE FIRST SHOT

**ON THE COVER: BOMBARDMENT FROM FORT JOHNSON, 1861.** Engravers at *Harper's Weekly* took Theodore Davis's sketch of the bombardment from Fort Johnson and created this engraving. (Fort Sumter National Monument Collections.)

IMAGES
*of America*

# THE FIRST SHOT

Robert N. Rosen and
Richard W. Hatcher III

ARCADIA
PUBLISHING

Published by Arcadia Publishing
Charleston, South Carolina

Printed in the United States of America

Library of Congress Control Number: 2010941810

For all general information, please contact Arcadia Publishing:
Telephone 843-853-2070
Fax 843-853-0044
E-mail sales@arcadiapublishing.com
For customer service and orders:
Toll-Free 1-888-313-2665

Visit us on the Internet at www.arcadiapublishing.com

# CONTENTS

# Note from the Authors

We are delighted to be able to present this short book on the first shot of the Civil War as part of the Lowcountry's observation of the war's sesquicentennial. Both of us have been active with the Fort Sumter–Fort Moultrie Historical Trust, which is working with various groups and organizations to coordinate events to commemorate the 150th anniversary of the Civil War. All of the royalties from the sale of this book will be donated to the trust, whose mission is to educate the public about Fort Sumter and Fort Moultrie and to support the National Park Service's efforts to preserve and protect the park sites and their resources for future generations.

We wish to thank Arcadia Publishing for working with the trust in this endeavor and for being a generous corporate citizen of the Lowcountry of South Carolina.

We believe this book is a good introduction to the beginning of the Civil War in Charleston. The trust is happy to work with schools, civic groups, and businesses to reprint copies of *The First Shot*, for promotional, advertising or educational purposes, as all royalties will go toward the educational activities of the trust for the sesquicentennial's commemoration. Please see our website at SCCivilWar.org.

—Robert N. Rosen and Richard W. Hatcher III
April 12, 2011

# ACKNOWLEDGMENTS

The authors wish to acknowledge the invaluable assistance of Mary G. Hatcher, who aided us in the selection of illustrations and the drafting of captions and text. We also wish to acknowledge the generous assistance of Fort Sumter National Monument, the South Carolina Historical Society, Middleton Place, the Renaissance Gallery, the Citadel, and the Washington Light Infantry. The support of Fort Sumter National Monument superintendent Bob Dodson and South Carolina Historical Society executive director Faye Jensen and assistant director John Tucker are greatly appreciated.

# INTRODUCTION

The Democratic Party's national convention was held in Charleston, South Carolina, in April 1860 to nominate a candidate for president and vice president of the United States. That convention deadlocked over the issue of slavery, and the Southern delegates walked out of Institute Hall on Meeting Street. When a friend asked Sen. Stephen A. Douglas of Illinois, the leading contender for the nomination, what he thought of the convention, Douglas replied: "Why, that men will be cutting one another's throats in a little while. In less than twelve months, we shall be at war and that the bloodiest in history."

The State of South Carolina seceded from the Union on December 20, 1860, at Institute Hall, the same hall that witnessed the collapse of the Democratic Party. Abraham Lincoln's election became a certainty. But James Buchanan remained president until Lincoln was inaugurated in March 1861.

Buchanan was president in December 1860, prior to the secession of South Carolina. He gave the impression that the federal government had accepted secession. For example, he seriously considered ordering Maj. Robert Anderson and his men to evacuate Fort Sumter and return to Fort Moultrie. "A President of the United States who would make such an order," his attorney general, Edwin Stanton, thundered, "would be guilty of treason." To which Buchanan replied, "Oh, no! Not so bad as that, my friend! Not so bad as that!" There was even a preliminary agreement to negotiate the ownership of federal property. He wrote in December 1860 "that if they [the Federal forts] were assailed this would put them completely in the wrong and making them the authors of the Civil War."

The North was in a state of anticipation. So was the South, and so were Charlestonians. On January 9, the *Star of the West*, a Union supply ship with 200 men bound for Fort Sumter, was turned back by Citadel cadets firing artillery from Morris Island and cannon fire from Fort Moultrie. "The expulsion of the *Star of the West* from Charleston Harbor yesterday morning was the opening of the ball of revolution," the *Charleston Mercury* crowed. "We are proud that our harbor has been so honored. We are more proud that the State of South Carolina, so long, so bitterly, so contemptuously reviled and scoffed at, above all others, should thus proudly have thrown back the scoff of her enemies." An officer on the *Star of the West* with a sense of humor said, "The people of Charleston pride themselves upon their hospitality, but it exceeded my expectations. They gave us several balls before we landed."

On February 24, one Charlestonian wrote, "Everybody apprehends that the *crisis* is approaching, that we are on the *eve* of an explosion." Many believed the South was bluffing. Pvt. John Thompson, stationed at Fort Sumter, wrote his father in Ireland, "You need not be in any unnecessary anxiety on my account, for to tell the truth in spite of all their bluster I am almost sure they never will fire a shot at us, indeed I think they are only too glad to be let alone."

Mrs. Thomas Smythe informed her son Augustine Smythe in a January 1861 letter that "the Northerners will have so much to do at home before long, they will be glad to let us alone. It is confidently predicted there will be no fighting of any magnitude in this region, nothing but skirmishing within sight of their boats."

Others, however, took the South at its word and began to prepare for civil war, even in the absence of strong presidential leadership. Sen. Simon Cameron of Pennsylvania was told that there was "one great consolidated party in favor of a fight and especially in favor of blotting out the city of Charleston." By then, even President Buchanan realized he could not just give away federal property. "If I withdraw Anderson from Sumter," he said, "I can travel home to Wheatland by the light of my own burning effigies."

The Confederate States of America was established on February 8, 1861. Lincoln was inaugurated on March 4. He promised in his inaugural address not to interfere with slavery but made it clear he would not brook secession: "In your hands, my dissatisfied fellow-countrymen, and not in mine, is the momentous issue of civil war. The government will not assail you. You can have no conflict without yourselves being the aggressors." Most Southerners interpreted Lincoln's address as the Charleston diarist Emma Holmes did: "stupid, ambiguous, vulgar and insolent," a "virtual declaration of war." The unadulterated Southern hatred for the new president knew no bounds. A reporter for the *Mercury* called him "the Ourang-Outang at the White House."

Major Anderson, the Union commander at Fort Sumter, who himself had been a slave owner and was married to a Georgian, gave the Confederates no cause for aggression. Indeed, Anderson himself, though loyal to the Union, accepted peaceful secession as inevitable and did all he could, consistent with his duty, to avert a war.

One could argue, as Milby Burton does in *The Siege of Charleston, 1861–1865*, that the first overt act of war was not the firing on Sumter but the seizing of Castle Pinckney, another federal fort in Charleston harbor. But federal forts had been taken by the Confederacy elsewhere. Or one could argue that the war started on January 9, 1861, with the firing on the *Star of the West*. Even Buchanan could not help but try to reprovision Sumter.

Occupying Fort Sumter through January, February, March, and the first part of April 1861, Anderson was a pawn in a larger game. Charleston was the stage, but the decisions were being made in Montgomery, the capital of the Confederacy, and in Washington. When asked by representatives of the Confederacy to surrender, Anderson politely refused. When Brig. Gen. P. G. T. Beauregard of Louisiana arrived to take charge of the Confederate military command at Charleston, the drama began.

The critical events of March and April 1861 are both obvious and mysterious. Did Lincoln cynically manipulate the Confederacy into firing the first shot, or did he bumble into the conflict while trying to preserve peace? Who, if anyone, was in control of the situation? What really happened?

In March 1861, when Lincoln became president, this was the lay of the land. Anderson was at Sumter. The Confederates occupied Fort Moultrie and Castle Pinckney. Only seven states (not including the key state of Virginia) had seceded. Three forts controlled by Federals lay in seceded territory: Fort Taylor in Key West, Fort Pickens in Pensacola, Florida, and Fort Sumter in Charleston harbor. By general consensus, North and South, Fort Sumter was to be the testing ground because it was a direct threat to Charleston, the Cradle of Secession. It was to be Abraham Lincoln's first test as president. In fact, as Kenneth Stampp has written, "Ever since December, Fort Sumter had seemed to be the place where war, if it came, would most likely begin."

This was Pres. Abraham Lincoln's dilemma: if he withdrew Union troops from Sumter, he would be acknowledging the actions of the South and the end of the Union. He would be yielding to force. He would be abandoning his oath to preserve, protect, and defend the Constitution of the United States. If he sent troops to defend Sumter, however, he would be the aggressor in a contest no one—North or South—wanted.

This was Pres. Jefferson Davis's dilemma: if the Union held Sumter, he would be acknowledging that he headed a government so weak that it allowed a foreign government to hold a fort in the harbor of its second-largest city. He would lose the respect and perhaps the recognition of foreign governments. On the other hand, an attack on a small band of soldiers who had given no provocation would be seen as unnecessarily aggressive and even cowardly. He would then be the warmonger. He would fire on the flag and cause millions of Northerners who did not want war to rally to Lincoln for a noble cause—the preservation of the Union.

The people of Charleston were looking to their new country and their new president for the right decision. Each side was evaluating the other. The Confederates wanted to take over Fort Sumter peaceably. Lincoln wanted to avoid a confrontation but maintain his position until something could be worked out. Supplies at Sumter were running low. It would take 20,000 Federal troops to hold the fort, according to Anderson. "Evacuation seems almost inevitable," wrote General-in-Chief Winfield Scott. Radical Republicans pushed Lincoln to start the war. Radical Confederates pushed Davis.

Could Lincoln have conceived of a plan during those months to force the issue at Charleston—to bring on the first shot by the Confederates—so that he could unify and rally Northern opinion? The evidence is very strong that he did.

On March 13, Capt. Gustavus V. Fox, a former naval officer and a trusted Lincoln lieutenant, presented a plan to Lincoln for a naval expedition to reinforce Fort Sumter. Fox came to Charleston on March 21, visited with Major Anderson, and told him of the possibility of such an expedition. Anderson did not like the idea. Fox also learned (and presumably told Lincoln) that Anderson could hold out only until April 15. Indeed, Anderson had written a letter in February describing how critical the situation was. The president had promised no interference at Sumter because he believed—erroneously—that Anderson could hold out. He had said so in his inaugural address. Now, literally the day after his inauguration, Lincoln read Anderson's letter and learned the truth. Sumter must be sent provisions or evacuated within a matter of weeks. Perhaps Lincoln wanted to wait. But he knew he could not wait much longer. Much of what the new president did next is shrouded in secrecy.

On March 21, Lincoln sent two other trusted friends to Charleston: Ward H. Lamon, a former law partner in Springfield and newly appointed federal marshal for the District of Columbia, and Stephen A. Hurlbut, also an Illinois lawyer and a Charleston native. Lamon wrote in his *Recollections* that he was sent on a confidential mission to the "virtual capital of the state which had been the pioneer in all of this haughty and stupendous work of rebellion." Lamon, described by Shelby Foote, the celebrated Civil War historian, as "a good man in a fight," was concerned for his physical safety: "I was about to trust my precious life and limbs as a stranger within her gates and an enemy to her cause." Secretary of State William Seward opposed Lamon's going to Charleston. According to Lamon's inflated recollections, Seward told Lincoln: "I greatly fear that you are sending Lamon to his grave. I fear they may kill him in Charleston. Those people are greatly excited, and are very desperate. We can't spare Lamon, and we shall feel very badly if anything serious should happen to him." "Mr. Secretary," replied Lincoln, "I have known Lamon to be in many a close place, and he has never been in one that he didn't get out of. By Jing! I'll risk him. Go Lamon, and God bless you! Bring back a Palmetto, if you can't bring us good news."

When Lamon arrived at the Charleston Hotel, he signed his name below the names of a group of Virginians and placed a long dash after it, giving any reader the erroneous impression that he was from Virginia.

On March 23, Lamon met with unionist James L. Petigru, who told him that peaceable secession or war was inevitable, that the "whole people were infuriated and crazed, and that no act of headlong violence by them would surprise him." He asked Lamon not to visit him again, "as every one who came near him was watched, and intercourse with him could only result in annoyance and danger to the visitor as well as to himself, and would fail to promote any good to the Union cause." It was now too late, he said.

Lamon also met with Gov. Francis Pickens, but not without incident. According to Lamon, the news had spread in Charleston that a "great Goliath from the North," a "Yankee Lincoln-hireling," had come to town uninvited. Thousands gathered at the hotel to catch a glimpse of this strange ambassador. The corridors, the main office, and the lobby were thronged, and the adjacent streets were crowded with people looking for a fight. The mood was ugly. "This was my initiation into the great 'Unpleasantness'," Lamon recalled. As he pressed his way through the crowd, he was touched on the shoulder by an elderly man who asked him in an authoritative tone of voice, "Are you Mark Lamon?" He replied, "No sir; I am Ward H. Lamon, at your service."

"Are you the man who registered here as Lamon, from Virginia?" the man asked. "I registered as Ward H. Lamon, without designating my place of residence. What is your business with me, sir?" "Oh, well," continued the man, "have you any objection to state what business you have here in Charleston?" "Yes, I have." Then after a pause, Lamon told the gentleman, "My business is with your governor, who is to see me as soon as he has finished his breakfast. If he chooses to impart to you my business in this city, you will know it; otherwise, not." The old gentleman then said, "Beg pardon; if you have business with our governor, it's all right; we'll see."

Shortly after breakfast, Lamon met with Governor Pickens, who told him in no uncertain terms that reinforcement of Fort Sumter meant war. "Nothing," he said, "can prevent war except acquiescence of the President of the United States in secession, and his unalterable resolve not to attempt any reinforcement of the Southern forts. To think of longer remaining in the Union is simply preposterous. We have five thousand well-armed soldiers around this city; all the States are arming with great rapidity; and this means war with all its consequences." Pickens concluded, "Let your President attempt to reinforce Sumter, and the tocsin of war will be sounded from every hill-top and valley in the South."

Lamon, for reasons that have never been clear, told Governor Pickens that Sumter would, in all probability, be abandoned, though he had no authority to give such assurances. Yet Lamon was as close a confidant and friend as Lincoln had. He had been Lincoln's law partner. It was Lamon who, armed with four pistols and two large knives, acted as Lincoln's personal bodyguard on his middle-of-the-night journey to Washington through Baltimore prior to assuming the presidency. Lamon next went to see a deeply despondent Major Anderson at Fort Sumter. The mob awaited Lamon's return to the Charleston Hotel, where he almost certainly would have been hurt, if not hanged, had it not been for the intercession of former congressman Lawrence Keitt, who happened on the scene.

After meeting with the local postmaster, Lamon took the night train back to Washington. Since he could not bring the president good news, he brought him back a palmetto branch. "I had ascertained the real temper and determination of their leaders by personal contact with them," he said, "and this made my mission one that was not altogether without profit to the great man at whose bidding I made the doubtful journey."

Lamon had left Governor Pickens with the distinct but erroneous impression that Sumter would be evacuated. Indeed, the whole country believed Sumter would be evacuated. Abner Doubleday later wrote, "Almost every one had persuaded himself that the new President would not attempt coercion." Lamon went even further after he departed Charleston and wrote to Governor Pickens to tell him that he would return to coordinate the evacuation. Either Lamon was part of a well-executed ploy by Lincoln; he acted on orders from Seward, who genuinely wanted to abandon Sumter; or he was simply young and impulsive. We will never know. Prof. Charles W. Ramsdell writes,

> What had he been sent to Charleston to do? There must have been some purpose and it could hardly have been to prepare the way for Anderson's evacuation. Does it strain the evidence to suggest that it was chiefly to find out at first hand how strong was the Southern feeling about relief for Fort Sumter and that this purpose was camouflaged by the vague intimation of evacuation?

Ramsdell argues that Lamon himself did not understand the real purpose of his visit because Lincoln would not have trusted his "bibulous and impulsive young friend" with such important information.

Stephen A. Hurlbut, later a major general in the Union army, conducted a quieter and more comprehensive investigation in Charleston for President Lincoln. A native Charlestonian, he came down on the train with his wife and Lamon but stayed with relatives. "On Sunday morning [March 27]," Hurlbut reported to Lincoln,

> I rode around the City, visiting especially the wharves and the Battery so as to view the shipping in port and the Harbour. I regret to say that no single vessel in port displayed American Colours. Foreign craft had their National Colors; the Flag of the Southern Confederacy, and of the State of South Carolina was visible every where—but the tall masts of Northern owned Ships were bare and showed no colors whatever. Four miles down the Harbor the Standard of the U. States floated over Fort Sumter, the only evidence of jurisdiction and nationality.

On Monday, March 25, Hurlbut met with Petigru, with whom he had studied law. Petigru told Hurlbut what he had told Lamon, that there was now not a drop of loyalty to the Union in South Carolina. He visited with merchants, businessmen, planters, old friends, and family. He attended church. "From these sources," Hurlbut concluded:

> I have no hesitation in reporting as unquestionable, that Separate Nationality is a fixed fact, that there is an unanimity of sentiment which to my mind is astonishing—that there is no attachment to the Union—that almost every one of those very men who in 1832 held military commissions under secret orders from Gen'l Jackson and were in fact ready to draw the sword in civil war for the Nation, are now as ready to take arms if necessary for the Southern Confederacy.

Charlestonians, Hurlbut noted, expected to gain a commercial advantage in the event of war. "They expect a golden era, when Charleston shall be a great Commercial Emporium and Control for the South as New York does for the North."

Hurlbut informed Lincoln on March 27,

> I have no doubt that a ship known to contain only provisions for Sumpter [sic] would be stopped and refused admittance. Even the moderate men who desire not to open fire, believe in the safer policy of time and Starvation. At present the garrison can be withdrawn without insult to them or their flag. In a week this may be impossible and probably will. If Sumpter is abandoned it is to a certain extent a concession of jurisdiction which cannot fail to have its effect at home and abroad.

Thus by March 27, when Lamon and Hurlbut returned to Washington, Lincoln knew that any attempt to relieve Sumter would result in war. He was also aware of a growing inclination in the North to fight for the Union. "I tell you, sir," an irate Republican wrote to one member of Lincoln's cabinet, "if Fort Sumter is evacuated, the new administration is done forever." A friend of John C. Breckinridge wrote, "Lincoln hesitates like an ass between two stacks of hay." Lincoln was also aware of the impatient and headstrong Governor Pickens of South Carolina, who was capable of starting the war with or without the Confederacy.

On March 29, Lincoln met with his cabinet, which was divided on the issue of Fort Sumter. Seward wrote at the time, "I do not think it wise to provoke a Civil War beginning at Charleston and in rescue of an untenable position." Lincoln, however, had made up his mind. He issued a secret order to prepare a naval expedition. Its destination was not given, but it was to sail on April 6, "to be used or not according to circumstances." Lincoln also made other preparations, so secret that they were kept from the Secretary of War and the Secretary of the Navy.

On April 4, Lincoln held a meeting with a number of Republican governors known to favor a strong stand at Sumter. No one knows what transpired at that meeting, though some historians conjecture that Lincoln told them of his plan and warned them to prepare for war. On the same day, he also met with John B. Baldwin, a Virginia unionist, who told the president that the only solution was to evacuate Fort Sumter. According to Baldwin's later sworn testimony before a Congressional committee, Lincoln became excited and said, "Why was I not told this a week ago? You have come too late!"

Actually, it was not too late. Still on April 4, Lincoln met with Captain Fox, his agent to command the naval expedition to Charleston harbor. Fox got his orders personally from President Lincoln. Anderson would be relieved, Lincoln told Fox, but Governor Pickens would be notified first, before Fox could arrive at Sumter. Members of the Cabinet objected to this notification, but it was a key element in Lincoln's plan. A letter was then sent to Anderson by regular mail notifying him of the relief expedition. That letter, written by Lincoln himself (although it was copied and signed by the Secretary of War) reads as follows:

> Sir: Your letter of the 1st instant occasions some anxiety to the President. On information of Captain Fox he had supposed you could hold out till the 15th instant without any great inconvenience and had prepared an expedition to relieve you before that period. Hoping still that you will be able to sustain yourself till the 11th or 12th instant, the expedition will go forward, and finding your flag flying, will attempt to provision you, and in case the effort is resisted will endeavor also to reinforce you.
>
> You will therefore hold out, if possible, till the arrival of the expedition. It is not, however, the intention of the President to subject your command to any danger or hardship beyond what in your judgment would be usual in military life, and he has entire confidence that you will act as becomes a patriot and a soldier, under all circumstances. Whenever, if at all, in your judgment, to save yourself and command, a capitulation becomes a necessity, you are authorized to make it.

On April 6, Lincoln wrote an unaddressed and unsigned message to Governor Pickens in his own handwriting. It was personally delivered to the governor by a trusted state department clerk, Robert Chew:

> I am directed by the President of the United States to notify you to expect an attempt will be made to supply Fort Sumter with provisions only; and that, if such an attempt be not resisted, no effort to throw in men, arms, or ammunition will be made without further notice, or in case of an attack upon the fort.

As numerous historians have pointed out, this crucial message was a masterpiece of ambiguity. Lincoln, the master of the English language, the most eloquent of public speakers, the author of the Gettysburg Address, drafted a message in his own hand because he knew that all parties would read it differently. Let the great Southern historian Charles W. Ramsdell explain:

> To the suspicious and apprehensive Confederates it did not merely give information that provisions would be sent to Anderson's garrison—which should be enough to bring about an attempt to take the fort—but it carried a threat that force would be used if the provisions were not allowed to be brought in. It was a direct challenge! How were the Southerners expected to react to this challenge? To Northern readers the same words meant only that the government was taking food to hungry men to whom it was under special obligation. Northern men would see no threat; they would understand only that their government did not propose to use force if it could be avoided.

Late on the night of April 6 and into the morning hours of April 7, one of the most mysterious episodes of all took place. The *Powhatan*, the flagship of the naval expedition, left New York under a new commander, Lt. David D. Porter. Lincoln had given command to Porter, but Secretary of

State Seward, after conferring with Lincoln at midnight, wired, "Deliver the *Powhatan* at once to Captain Mercer." Porter apparently had other orders. He replied, "Have received confidential orders from the president and shall obey them." Was Porter under secret orders from Lincoln *not* to go to Sumter and thereby ensure that no attack would take place? Fox could not relieve Sumter without the powerful *Powhatan*. Or was Porter really ordered to proceed to Fort Pickens, not Sumter, because there was a mix-up between Seward and Lincoln? Secretary of the Navy Gideon Welles later claimed that Seward deliberately ruined Fox's relief expedition because he was embarrassed at having secretly promised prominent Southerners that Sumter would be evacuated and now could not deliver on his promise. We will never know. The great historians who have studied the matter in detail disagree.

On April 8, Lincoln's message was given to Governor Pickens and General Beauregard. At the same time, however, the Confederates already knew from intelligence and even newspaper reports that a large naval expedition was on its way. Theoretically, no one knew the destination of Captain Fox's seven ships, but Lincoln's message had implied that force would be available, and Fox's expedition must be that force. In fact, some of the ships were heading to Pensacola, but that was kept so secret that the Confederates assumed incorrectly that the entire expedition was headed for Charleston. On the same day, Major Anderson began to see the heavy artillery increase around him. A house on Sullivan's Island was torn down, revealing a battery of four powerful cannons.

The decision was now Jefferson Davis's to make. Both alternatives were dangerous. Either Fort Sumter must be captured before the Federal naval expedition arrived or it would be relieved by the Federal fleet. It was a Hobson's choice: if Sumter were attacked, the South would be the aggressor and would be put in the wrong. If Sumter were relieved, Davis's government would lose face. The Confederate Secretary of State, Robert Toombs, was against attacking Sumter. On the arrival of the telegram bearing Lincoln's notification to Governor Pickens, Toombs is reported to have said, "The firing upon that fort will inaugurate a civil war greater than any the world has yet seen." He told Jefferson Davis, "Mr. President, at this time it is suicide, murder, and will lose us every friend at the North. You will wantonly strike a hornet's nest which extends from mountains to ocean and legions now quiet will swarm out and sting us to death. It is unnecessary; it puts us in the wrong; it is fatal."

The historian Bruce Catton wrote, "It would be hard to put, in one paragraph, a better explanation of the tactical insight behind Lincoln's decision to send Captain Fox down to Charleston harbor."

But what could Jefferson Davis do? If he allowed Lincoln to reprovision Fort Sumter peaceably, Lincoln might then give him "further notice" that he was throwing in "men, arms, or ammunition." Had not the message clearly said so? On Davis's instruction, Confederate Secretary of War Leroy Pope Walker telegraphed Beauregard, "Under no circumstances are you to allow provisions to be sent to Fort Sumter."

On April 9, Beauregard discovered by seizing the mail from Fort Sumter that Anderson knew of the arrival of the Federal fleet. Indeed, the public knew all about the so-called secret preparation for war from the New York newspapers, which printed lurid and fairly accurate accounts of various ships' and troops' movements. The *Mercury* printed detailed accounts from the New York papers on April 10. Also on April 10, the Confederate government learned definitely that the naval expedition had left New York, and it decided to act before the fleet could arrive. Time was now a decisive factor. Beauregard was ordered to proceed. "The gage is thrown down," said the *Charleston Mercury*, "and we accept the challenge. We will meet the invader, and God and Battle must decide the issue between the hirelings of Abolition hate and Northern tyranny, and the people of South Carolina defending their freedom and their homes."

Mary Chesnut confided to her diary:

> Companies & regiments come constantly in. [Col. Louis T.] Wigfall all night in the harbor. Anderson burning blue lights as signals to the fleet. . . . Mr. Chesnut [Col.

James Chesnut Jr.] has gone in some sort of uniform, sash & sword, to demand the surrender of Fort Sumter. Patience oh my soul—if Anderson will not surrender, to night the bombardment begins. Have mercy upon us, Oh Lord! . . . If I could but know the answer of Anderson. They have intercepted a letter from him urging them to let him evacuate—painting very strongly the horrors likely to ensure. Poor country—with such rulers.—

Beauregard brought in 5,000 more soldiers because he felt that the Yankees were on the way to land troops and attack Morris Island. He determined to build a "circle of fire" around Fort Sumter. Efforts were redoubled. General Beauregard told Confederate Secretary of War Walker that "if Sumter was properly garrisoned and armed, it would be a perfect Gibraltar to anything but constant shelling, night and day, from the four points of the compass. As it is, the weakness of the garrison constitutes our greatest advantage, and we must, for the present, turn our attention to preventing it from being re-enforced." Private Thompson described the situation inside Fort Sumter:

> Our supply of breadstuffs was fast giving out and the Carolinians knew it. They had cut off all communication with the shore, and starvation was staring us in the face. We had been on 3/4 rations for a long time and on the 8th of April a reduction to half rations was made and cheerfully submitted to, the hope of being re-enforced or withdrawn having not yet entirely left us. On the eleventh one biscuit was our allowance, and matters seemed rapidly coming to a crisis.

The 2,000 men at Morris Island scurried around in anticipation. More than 6,000 Confederate troops surrounded the small band at Fort Sumter. The *Courier* editorialized: "We are sick of the subject of evacuation. . . . Let the strife begin." The city was crowded with soldiers, wagons, horses, and people waiting for the war to start. The harbor was full of boats transporting troops. On April 11, Beauregard learned that one of Fox's ships was only a few miles away. That afternoon, Col. James Chesnut Jr. and Capt. Stephen D. Lee went to Sumter to hand Anderson a message from Beauregard. "I am ordered by the Government of the Confederate States," it read, "to demand the evacuation of Fort Sumter." Anderson replied that the demand to evacuate was one with which "I regret that my sense of honor, and of my obligations to my Government, prevent my compliance." When Anderson asked if he would be notified prior to the commencement of firing, he was told that he would. "I shall wait the first shot," Anderson replied, "and if you do not batter us to pieces, we shall be starved out in a few days."

Anderson's remarks were reported to Beauregard, who wired Montgomery for instructions. The instructions were to obtain from Major Anderson a fixed time for his surrender. Still anxious to avoid bloodshed, Beauregard sent his aides out to Anderson again after midnight to inquire as to when Anderson would be "starved out"—and could then honorably surrender. Beauregard had been Anderson's student at West Point, and he showed his former professor every courtesy. Anderson played for time, knowing the fleet was on its way. Finally he replied that he would evacuate on April 15 at noon (as his men would have been without food for three days by then), "should I not receive prior to that time controlling instructions from my Government or additional supplies." But the Montgomery government had already telegraphed Beauregard,

> Do not desire needlessly to bombard Fort Sumter. If Major Anderson will state the time at which . . . he will evacuate, and agree that in the meantime he will not use his guns against us unless ours should be employed against Fort Sumter, you are authorized thus to avoid the effusion of blood. If this or its equivalent be refused, reduce the fort.

Colonel Chesnut, Beauregard's aid, knowing also that the fleet was on the way, could not agree to any further delay. He had waited too long already at Sumter for Anderson's reply. Indeed, Chesnut sincerely believed this was all a political charade and that there would be no war. In November, he had said that "the man most averse to blood might safely drink every drop shed in establishing a Southern Confederacy." As he stood at Fort Sumter, he wrote to Anderson as follows:

> Fort Sumter, S.C., April 12, 1861, 3:20 A.M. Sir: By authority of Brigadier General Beauregard, commanding the Provisional Forces of the Confederate States, we have the honor to notify you that he will open the fire of his batteries on Fort Sumter in one hour from this time. We have the honor to be very respectfully, Your obedient servants, James Chesnut, Jr., Aide-de-camp. Stephen D. Lee, Captain C.S. Army, Aid-de-camp.

It was 3:30 a.m., April 12, 1861. According to Capt. Stephen D. Lee, another of Beauregard's aides who accompanied Chesnut, Anderson seemed to realize the importance of the consequences and the great responsibility of his position. He told the Confederate officers, "If we never meet in this world again, God grant that we may meet in the next." The war that no one wanted, that no one really believed would ever happen, was about to begin.

The bombardment of Fort Sumter, a truly glorious spectacle were it not so imbued with tragedy, began at 4:30 on the morning of April 12. It was a cloudy morning. Not a star was visible. A heavy mist covered the harbor and the adjacent islands. Through that gloom, one contemporary eyewitness wrote, "came the brilliant flash of exploding shells from the batteries all around the bay, while the deep hoarse tones of talking cannon echoed over the waters, the scene was sublimely grand, and sensations wildly inspiriting swelled in every heart." Three Union vessels remained outside the bar, unable and to all appearances unwilling to enter the harbor.

Colonel Chesnut and his fellow officers had left Fort Sumter and gone to Fort Johnson on James Island. There either Chesnut or Lee gave Capt. George S. James the order to fire. The first mortar shot arched high into the air and exploded over Fort Sumter. It was the signal to start the Civil War. The second shot was also fired from Fort Johnson, this one by Lt. W. H. Gibbes of Columbia. Tradition has it, incorrectly, that the first shot of the war was fired by Edmund Ruffin of Virginia, the 67-year-old radical secessionist, writer, agriculturist, and fanatic. Ruffin came to Charleston to avoid being "under his [Lincoln's] government even for an hour." In fact, Ruffin pulled the lanyard of a Columbiad gun at the Iron Battery on Cummings Point, Morris Island. It was a direct hit against the parapet of Fort Sumter. Abner Doubleday wrote that a shot from Cummings Point "lodged in the magazine wall, and by the sound seemed to bury itself in the masonry about a foot from my head, in very unpleasant proximity to my right ear. This is the one that probably came with Mr. Ruffin's compliments." Ruffin fired the first shot from Cummings Point, but it was Lt. Henry S. Farley who pulled the lanyard on the signal shot. Roger Pryor of Virginia, who had urged the Charlestonians to "strike a blow," could not bring himself to fire the first shot of the war when the opportunity was offered to him. In later years, no one disputed Ruffin's claim in his diary that he had fired the first shot of the Civil War.

All of the forts in the harbor then commenced firing. "At half past four [I heard] the heavy booming of cannon," Mary Chesnut wrote. "I sprang out of bed, and on my knees prostrate, I prayed as I never prayed before." By 5:00 a.m., more than 40 cannons were firing on Sumter from two batteries on James Island (including Fort Johnson), three on Cummings Point on Morris Island, a battery in Mount Pleasant, and four batteries on Sullivan's Island (including Fort Moultrie). Shots were not fired from the Battery in Charleston.

The bombardment was furious. It was constant for the first two and a half hours. "There stands the bold defiant fort," F. L. Parker wrote, "as quiet as death. No light is seen, not a sign of life appears, not even a sentinel can be distinguished, but high above her floats her proud banner, the Stars and Stripes, the flag which for 75 years has never quailed before an enemy."

Private Thompson described the situation inside Sumter:

> At 3 o'clock we hoisted our colors the glorious "Star Spangled Banner" and quietly awaited the enemies fire. Long before daylight, at 4 1/2 A.M., the first shell came hissing

through the air and burst right over our heads. The thrill that ran through our veins at this time was indescribable, none were afraid, the stern defiant look on each man's countenance plainly told that fear was no part of his constitution, but something like an expression of awe crept over the features of everyone, as battery after battery opened fire and the hissing shot came plowing along leaving wreck and ruin in their path.

After daybreak, the defenders of Fort Sumter fought back and fought bravely, but they were no match for Beauregard's artillery. Charlestonians climbed onto rooftops to watch the attack and cheer on the Confederacy. The Battery and all the wharves were crowded with spectators. The sounds of the cannons were loud and terrifying. Shot poured into the fort in an incessant stream, causing great flakes of masonry to fall in all directions. Giant mortar shells, after sailing high in the air, landed in the parade ground of Sumter, and their explosion shook the fort like an earthquake. Houses and buildings in the old city rattled. Abner Doubleday claims to have fired the first shot on behalf of the Union forces: "In aiming the first gun fired against the rebellion I had no feeling of self-reproach, for I fully believed that the contest was inevitable, and was not of our seeking." Private Thompson wrote,

> Towards mid-day we could distinctly see a fleet of three war vessels off the bay, and we were certain they were an expedition fitted out to relieve us, and the hopes of speedily getting assistance compensated for the lack of anything in the shape of dinner. . . . We confidently expected the fleet to make some attempt to land supplies and re-enforcements during the night, it being as dark as pitch and raining, but we were disappointed. Morning dawned and with appetites unappeased and haggard look, although determined and confident, all took their positions for the day's work.

The bombardment continued into Saturday, April 13. "Hot shot" was hurled into Sumter. The troops there continued to fire back. "I witnessed then a scene that I doubt was ever equaled," the Reverend A. Toomer Porter wrote. "The gallantry of the defense struck the chivalry of the attackers, and without a command every soldier mounted the parapet of every battery of the Confederates and gave three cheers for Major Anderson." Beauregard too later reported that the Confederate troops, "carried away by their natural generous impulses, mounted the different batteries, and . . . cheered the garrison for its pluck and gallantry and hooted the fleet lying inactive just outside the bar."

The "hot shot" had its effect: the building inside Sumter caught fire. "The heat and smoke inside was awful," a Union soldier later recalled. "The only way to breathe was to lay flat on the ground and keep your face covered with a wet handkerchief." Anderson could not hold out, and the fleet led by Fox did not come to his rescue. "Part of the fleet was visible outside the bar about half-past ten A.M. It exchanged salutes with us," a Union officer wrote, "but did not attempt to enter the harbor, or take part in the battle. In fact, it would have had considerable difficulty in finding the channel as the marks and buoys had all been taken up."

On April 14, Anderson surrendered. Remarkably, there were no deaths and only a few wounded. The local news reports were thrilling:

> The advantage was unquestionably upon the side of Fort Moultrie. In that fort not a gun was dismounted, not a wound received, not the slightest permanent injury sustained by any of its defenses, while every ball from Fort Moultrie left its mark upon Fort Sumter. . . . The last two or three hours before dark, Major Anderson devoted himself exclusively to Fort Moultrie, and the two fortresses had a grand duello. Game to the last, though much more exposed, Fort Moultrie held her own, and it is believed, a little more than her own. Towards night, several rounds of red-hot shot were thrown into the barracks of the enemy.

Beauregard sent over a fire engine from the city. The Stars and Stripes were lowered. Captain Doubleday made preparations to fire a salute to the American flag. It was a dangerous thing to attempt as sparks of fire were floating around everywhere, and there was no safe place to deposit the blank cartridges. Unfortunately, on the 43rd round of a planned 100-gun salute, the cannon fired prematurely and blew off the right arm of the gunner, Daniel Hough, killing him almost instantaneously. He was the first soldier to die for the Union in the Civil War.

"About eighteen hundred shots had been fired into Fort Sumter," wrote Doubleday, "and the upper story was pretty well knocked to pieces. To walk around the parapet we had constantly to climb over heaps of debris." The fort was taken. The *Mercury* exalted:

> The rest is briefly told. Col. Wigfall returned and notified the captains of the several companies to inform their respective commands that the fort was unconditionally surrendered. The scene that followed was altogether indescribable. The troops upon the hills cheered and cheered again. A horseman galloped at full speed along the beach, waving his cap to the troops near the lighthouse. These soon caught up the cry, and the whole shore rang with the glad shouts of thousands.

Charleston and the Confederacy celebrated. The harbor was soon filled with boats. Charlestonians wanted to see the results of the first battle of the Civil War.

Yet in truth the victory belonged to a man far away from Charleston, Abraham Lincoln. His strategy had worked. He had forced the Confederacy to fire at Fort Sumter, thereby electrifying the North. The "time before Sumter was like another century," wrote a New York woman. "It seems as if we never were alive till now; never had a country till now." Public opinion in the North, once divided, now united behind the president. "The first gun that spat its iron insult at Fort Sumter," declared Oliver Wendell Holmes in an 1863 Fourth of July oration in Boston, "smote every loyal American full in the face." The president had only tried to send food to loyal starving soldiers. The rebels had opened fire on a Federal fort for no reason. On May 1, Lincoln wrote to Fox:

> You and I both anticipated that the cause of the country would be advanced by making the attempt to provision Fort Sumter, even if it should fail; and it is no small consolation now to feel that our anticipation is justified by the result.

Lincoln's two secretaries, John G. Nicolay and John Hay, wrote later:

> President Lincoln in deciding the Sumter question had adopted a simple but effective policy. To use his own words, he determined to "send bread to Anderson"; if the rebels fired on that, they would not be able to convince the world that he had begun the civil war.

And Lincoln himself told his trusted friend Orville H. Browning of his plan later that year, in July. Browning recorded his conversation with Lincoln as follows:

> He himself conceived the idea, and proposed sending supplies, without an attempt to reinforce giving notice of the fact to Gov. Pickens of S.C. The plan succeeded. They attacked Sumter—it fell, and thus, did more service than it otherwise could.

A former Union officer stationed at Fort Sumter in April 1861, Dr. Samuel W. Crawford, later wrote a history of the events he had witnessed, *The Genesis of the Civil War*. He concluded that Lincoln had indeed maneuvered the Confederacy into firing the first shot:

> The action of the Montgomery Cabinet was unavoidable and, in a manner, forced upon it. The current of events had set manifestly towards the near commencement of

hostilities, but it was hoped by those in favor of a peaceful settlement that something might yet be gained by delay. A large number of influential men had not yet defined their position. In the harbor of Charleston, the preparations for an attack were not complete, and the Confederate Commissioners were yet in Washington. But the communication of the President precipitated the issue and forced it to an unavoidable conclusion. The temper of South Carolina was well known.

Indeed, the temper of Charlestonians was well known. They were ecstatic.

"The streets of Charleston present some such aspect as those of Paris in the last revolution," William Howard Russell wrote in *My Diary, North & South*:

> Crowds of armed men singing and promenading the streets. The battle-blood running through their veins—that hot oxygen which is called "the flush of victory" on the cheek; restaurants full, reveling in barrooms, club-rooms crowded, orgies and carousing in tavern or private house, in taproom, from cabaret—down narrow alleys, in the broad highway. Sumter has set them distraught; never was such a victory; never such brave lads; never such a fight.

*     *     *

In his 1898 memoir, the Reverend A. Toomer Porter, a Charleston Episcopal priest, related a conversation he had with Col. James Chesnut at the Battery several months before the first shot. "These are troublous times, Colonel," Toomer said. "We are at the beginning of a terrible war." Chesnut replied, "Not all, there will be no war, it will be all arranged. I will drink all the blood in the war."

Toomer concluded: "So little did some of our leaders realize the awful import of what we were doing."

**C. 1863 PRINT OF THE APRIL 12–13, 1861, BOMBARDMENT OF FORT SUMTER.** Upon receiving the news of the bombardment of Fort Sumter, illustrators produced a flood of prints and engravings depicting this momentous event. These images appeared in myriad newspapers, periodicals, magazines, and books of the era. (Fort Sumter National Monument Collections.)

**CHARLESTON, 1855.** The most important shipping port on the U.S. South Atlantic coast, Charleston's 1860 population was 40,578 (white, slave, and free black). It was the second largest city in the Deep South (New Orleans, Louisiana, was the largest). (*Ballou's Pictorial*, March 24, 1855. Fort Sumter National Monument Collections.)

**1860 Photograph of the Battery.** White Point Gardens, more famously known as "the Battery," earned that name for the cannons placed there during the War of 1812. With its open space and unobstructed view of the harbor, the park quickly became the gathering point for Charlestonians to witness the bombardment of Fort Sumter (U.S. Army Heritage and Education Center.)

**C. 1860–1861 PHOTOGRAPH SHOWING THE CIRCULAR CONGREGATIONAL CHURCH AND THE SOUTH CAROLINA INSTITUTE HALL.** It was at Institute Hall where the Democratic Party National Convention met in April 1860. When the delegates from the Deep South walked out of the convention, it signaled the collapse of the nation's two-party system and the real beginning of the breakup of the Union. Both buildings perished in the Great Fire of December 1861. (South Carolina Historical Society Collections.)

**1865 Photograph from the Roof of the Orphan Asylum, Looking East toward Charleston Harbor.** This image, though taken after the war, provides a view much like one that would be seen in 1860–1861. (Library of Congress.)

PALMETTO-TREE, AND OLD CUSTOM-HOUSE, AT CHARLEST

UTH CAROLINA.

DECEMBER 1, 1860,
*HARPER'S WEEKLY* PRINT
OF A STREET SCENE
IN CHARLESTON WITH
THE OLD EXCHANGE
BUILDING (CUSTOMS
HOUSE) IN THE
BACKGROUND. The Old
Exchange Building is a
pre–Revolutionary War
government building
that was used for a
variety of purposes. It
was the site of South
Carolina's ratification of
the U.S. Constitution
in 1788 and served both
as a United States and
Confederate post office.
(Fort Sumter National
Monument Collections.)

**1860–1861 VIEW OF CHARLESTON FROM CASTLE PINCKNEY'S PARAPET.** The two people in the sketch are probably Sgt. James Skillen, of the U.S. Ordnance Department, and his daughter Katherine. Skillen served as "Fort Keeper," providing basic maintenance and security of the fortification. The sergeant and his daughter comprised Castle Pinckney's "garrison" until early December 1860, when an army officer and small civilian workforce arrived at the fortification to make repairs. (*Battles and Leaders of the Civil War.*)

**CHARLESTONIANS GATHERED AT HIBERNIAN HALL.** Hibernian Hall and the Mills House (to the right in the illustration) both provided lodging for delegates to the 1860 Democratic National Convention, held at Institute Hall, only a block away. (*Frank Leslie's Illustrated Newspaper*, December 1, 1860. Fort Sumter National Monument Collections.)

**SOUTH CAROLINA INSTITUTE HALL.** Home of the contentious Democratic National Convention from April 23 to May 3, 1860, the hall once again became the focus of national attention eight months later in December as the site where delegates signed the Ordinance of Secession. It then became known as Secession Hall. (*Harper's Weekly*, April 21, 1860. Fort Sumter National Monument Collections.)

THE NATIONAL DEMOCRATIC NOMINATING CONVENTION IN SESSION AT CHARLESTON, SOUTH CAR

ON APRIL 23, 1860.—[FROM A SKETCH BY OUR ARTIST CORRESPONDENT.]

SCENE INSIDE SOUTH CAROLINA INSTITUTE HALL DURING THE DEMOCRATIC NATIONAL CONVENTION IN APRIL 1860. The Charleston Hotel was home to the ultra-Southern, "fire-eating" secessionist delegates. Symbolically, these delegates chose to stay at the opposite end of Meeting Street from the moderate Stephen Douglas delegates lodged at the Mills House and Hibernian Hall. (*Harper's Weekly*, April 28, 1860. Fort Sumter National Monument Collections.)

**ABRAHAM LINCOLN.** This photograph was made from a negative taken in Springfield, Illinois, on June 3, 1860, about two weeks after he won the Republican nomination for president. (Library of Congress.)

**CROWD GATHERED AT CITY HALL IN CHARLESTON IN NOVEMBER 1860.** When the news of Abraham Lincoln's election to the presidency was announced, Southerners were outraged. Lincoln's determination to restrict slavery to those areas of the United States where it already existed inflamed most Charlestonians, who considered it a virtual declaration of war. (*Frank Leslie's Illustrated Newspaper*, November 24, 1860. Fort Sumter National Monument Collections.)

# CHARLESTON
# MERCURY
## EXTRA:

Passed unanimously at 1.15 o'clock, P. M. December 20th, 1860.

### AN ORDINANCE

*To dissolve the Union between the State of South Carolina and other States united with her under the compact entitled " The Constitution of the United States of America."*

*We, the People of the State of South Carolina, in Convention assembled, do declare and ordain, and it is hereby declared and ordained,*

That the Ordinance adopted by us in Convention, on the twenty-third day of May, in the year of our Lord one thousand seven hundred and eighty-eight, whereby the Constitution of the United States of America was ratified, and also, all Acts and parts of Acts of the General Assembly of this State, ratifying amendments of the said Constitution, are hereby repealed; and that the union now subsisting between South Carolina and other States, under the name of " The United States of America," is hereby dissolved.

# THE
# UNION
# IS
# DISSOLVED!

"THE UNION IS DISSOLVED." This *Charleston Mercury* broadside is the most important newspaper flyer in Charleston's history and perhaps in U.S. history. The *Charleston Mercury*, long a proponent of secession, had this "extra" on the streets literally within five minutes of the enactment of the Ordinance of Secession. The *Mercury* announcement appears in virtually every pictorial history of the Civil War. (South Carolina Historical Society Collections.)

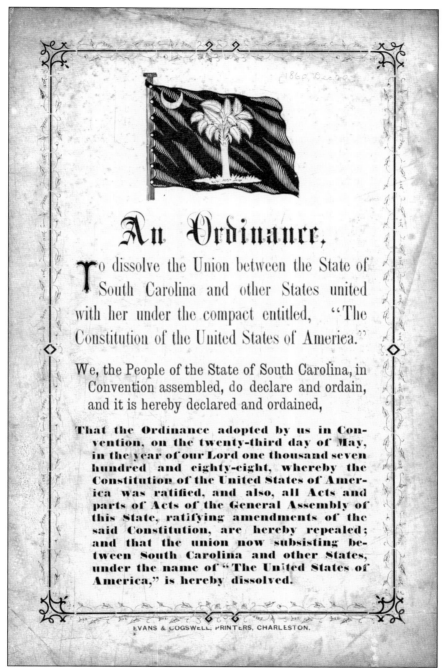

# An Ordinance,

To dissolve the Union between the State of South Carolina and other States united with her under the compact entitled, "The Constitution of the United States of America."

We, the People of the State of South Carolina, in Convention assembled, do declare and ordain, and it is hereby declared and ordained,

That the Ordinance adopted by us in Convention, on the twenty-third day of May, in the year of our Lord one thousand seven hundred and eighty-eight, whereby the Constitution of the United States of America was ratified, and also, all Acts and parts of Acts of the General Assembly of this State, ratifying amendments of the said Constitution, are hereby repealed; and that the union now subsisting between South Carolina and other States, under the name of "The United States of America," is hereby dissolved.

EVANS & COGSWELL, PRINTERS, CHARLESTON.

THE ORDINANCE OF SECESSION. The Ordinance of Secession was transcribed and printed in pamphlet form by Evans & Cogswell of Charleston in 1861. They were offered for sale to the public. Prior to secession, there was no official South Carolina flag, but on January 28, 1861, the legislature meeting in Hibernian Hall passed the bill establishing a flag for the "republic." Note the crescent on the flag with the horns up; it was not until 1910 that the crescent was turned as it appears today. (Library of Congress.)

**NOVEMBER 12, 1860, INSTITUTE HALL MEETING.** The mass meeting held in Institute Hall on November 12, 1860, called for the South Carolina legislature to hold a state convention to "discuss the question of secession from the Union." Approximately five weeks later, on December 20,

another excited crowd gathered in Institute Hall and witnessed the state's secession. (*Frank Leslie's Illustrated Newspaper*, November 24, 1860. Fort Sumter National Monument Collections.)

**TRANSFER OF THE UNION GARRISON TO FORT SUMTER.** On the night of December 26, 1860, Maj. Robert Anderson transferred his command from Fort Moultrie to Fort Sumter. In a report to Washington concerning the move, he wrote, "The step which I have taken was, in my opinion, necessary to prevent the effusion of blood." (*Frank Leslie's Illustrated Newspaper*, January 16, 1861. Fort Sumter National Monument Collections.)

**DISABLING THE GUNS AT FORT MOULTRIE.** As the U.S. garrison prepared to leave Fort Moultrie and move to Fort Sumter, they spiked the guns. The men of the garrison drove a spike ("a jagged and hardened steel spike with a soft point, or a nail without a head," as defined by Col. H. L. Scott in his 1864 *Military Dictionary*) into the vent (touch hole) of each of the guns. The spike was then "broken off flush with the outer surface" of the barrel, and the portion within the bore was then bent back using the rammer. (*Frank Leslie's Illustrated Newspaper*, January 5, 1861. Fort Sumter National Monument Collections.)

**CUTTING DOWN THE FLAGPOLE.** In addition to spiking Fort Moultrie's cannons, Anderson's men also cut down the flagpole so it could not be used by South Carolinians to fly their flag once they occupied the fort. (*Frank Leslie's Illustrated Newspaper*, January 19, 1861. Fort Sumter National Monument Collections.)

**FIRING THE CARRIAGES.** When Anderson moved his command from Fort Moultrie to Fort Sumter, the wooden cannon carriages facing Fort Sumter were set on fire to prevent their use against Fort Sumter. (*Harper's Weekly*, January 26, 1861. Fort Sumter National Monument Collections.)

**FORT MOULTRIE, NIGHT OF DECEMBER 26, 1860.** Artistic license was used in this depiction of Fort Moultrie showing all the gun carriages on fire and the U.S. flag still flying after Major Anderson transferred his command to Fort Sumter that night. In reality, only those guns carriages facing Fort Sumter were burned, the U.S. flag was taken to Fort Sumter, and the flagpole was cut down. (*Frank Leslie's Illustrated Newspaper*, January 5, 1861. Fort Sumter National Monument Collections.)

**ANDERSON'S COMMAND ARRIVING AT FORT SUMTER ON THE NIGHT OF DECEMBER 26, 1860.**
The Federals quickly moved in and secured the fort, which was still under construction. A group of civilian workers employed by the U.S. Army Corps of Engineers were at the fort, most from Charleston and pro-secession. These men were placed in boats and sent to the city. However, 40 workers who were pro-Union and from Baltimore volunteered to stay and help prepare Fort Sumter's defenses. (*Harper's Weekly*, January 12, 1861. Fort Sumter National Monument Collections.)

**RAISING THE U.S. FLAG AT SUMTER, DECEMBER 27, 1860.** At 11:45 a.m., the Federals gathered on Fort Sumter's parade ground to raise the U.S. colors. After a prayer by Chaplain Matthias Harris, Major Anderson, who was kneeling, rose and raised the flag. From the parapet, the regimental band played "the National air." One account states "Hail Columbia," was played, while another states it was "The Star Spangled Banner." "The Star Spangled Banner" did not become the national anthem until 1931. (*Frank Leslie's Illustrated Newspaper*, January 26, 1861. Fort Sumter National Monument Collections.)

**TEN-INCH COLUMBIAD MOUNTED ON THE PARADE GROUND AT FORT SUMTER.** When Anderson and his command arrived at Fort Sumter, there were already 15 cannons mounted. By April 12, 1861, a total of 46 more were ready for action. This February 16, 1861, *Harper's Weekly* illustration

shows a 10-inch Columbiad mounted as a mortar to fire on Charleston. However, the gun was not used during the bombardment. (Fort Sumter National Monument Collections.)

**INTERIOR OF ONE OF THE OFFICERS' QUARTERS, FORT SUMTER.** The tranquility depicted in the illustration is at odds with the extreme political and military tension that existed in the

winter of 1861 with Fort Sumter in the eye of the approaching storm. (Fort Sumter National Monument Collections).

**THE MAIN BATTERY AT FORT SUMTER.** These guns, located in the fort's right face first tier casemates, faced Fort Moultrie on Sullivan's Island and saw action during the April 12–13, 1861, bombardment. (*Harper's Weekly*, January 26, 1861. Fort Sumter National Monument Collections.)

**Guns in First Tier Casemates at Fort Sumter.** This is the only known photograph showing guns in Fort Sumter's first tier casemates. (South Carolina Historical Society Collections.)

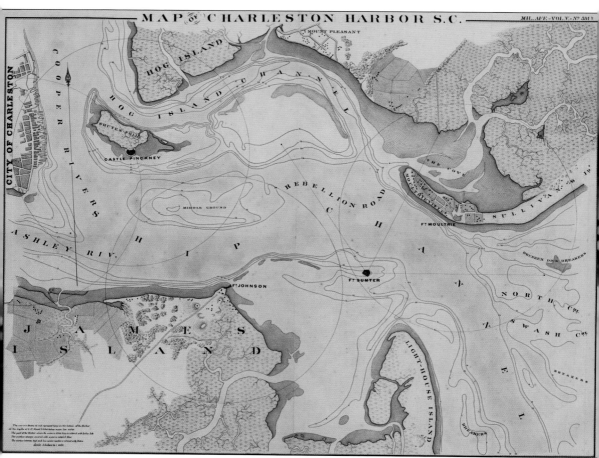

**MAP OF FORTIFICATIONS IN CHARLESTON HARBOR AT THE TIME OF SOUTH CAROLINA'S SECESSION.** At the time of secession, Fort Sumter was still incomplete; Castle Pinckney was under the supervision of a lone sergeant; Fort Johnson had been abandoned since the mid-1820s; and Fort Moultrie, under the command of Maj. Robert Anderson, maintained only a small garrison. (Library of Congress.)

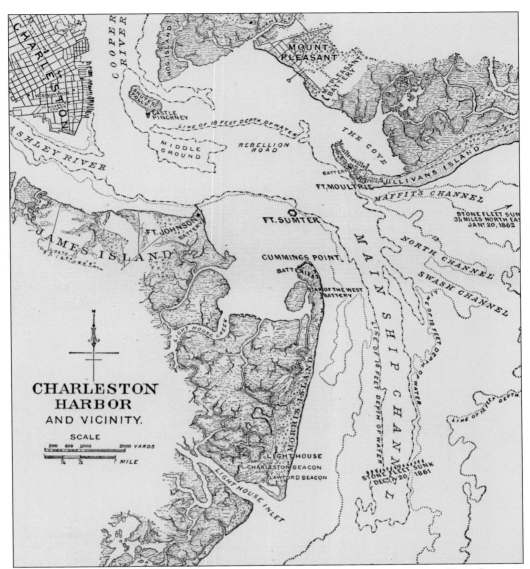

MAP OF THE CONFEDERATES' HARBOR DEFENSES, INCLUDING THOSE THAT FIRED ON FORT SUMTER, APRIL 12–13, 1861. Forty-three Confederate guns and mortars fired on Fort Sumter from every compass point around Charleston harbor—north at Mount Pleasant, south at Cummings Point, east at Sullivan's Island, and west near Fort Johnson. (*Battles and Leaders of the Civil War.*)

**CASTLE PINCKNEY.** Once Gov. Francis Pickens learned on December 27, 1860, that Maj. Robert Anderson had moved his command from Fort Moultrie to Fort Sumter, he ordered state militia to take control of Castle Pinckney, Fort Moultrie, Fort Johnson, and the U.S. (Charleston) Arsenal. Detachments from the Washington Light Infantry, Meagher Guards, and Carolina Light Infantry

composed the command that landed around 4:00 p.m. and took the fortification without incident. It became the first U.S. military installation taken by troops from a seceded state. (*Harper's Weekly*, January 12, 1861. Fort Sumter National Monument Collections.)

**Francis W. Pickens.** Before being elected South Carolina's governor on December 12, 1860, Pickens had been an attorney and planter, served in the state legislature and U.S. Congress, and from 1858 to 1860 was ambassador to Russia. Mary Boykin Chesnut named him "a fire-eater down to the ground." (*Battles and Leaders of the Civil War.*)

THE SUMTER GARRISON WATCHING THE FIRING ON THE "STAR OF THE WEST."

**FIRING ON THE *STAR OF THE WEST*, JANUARY 9, 1861.** This drawing by Theodore R. Davis, an artist for *Harper's Weekly*, was made during his tour of Charleston in April and May 1861, two days after the surrender of Fort Sumter and months after the actual firing on the *Star of the West*. Davis, then 21 years old, claimed to be an illustrator for the *Illustrated London News* and traveled with William Howard Russell of the London *Times*. He fooled the Southerners (who would not have cooperated with a Yankee journal like *Harper's Weekly*) and Russell as well. The drawing depicts the Union garrison at Fort Sumter, unable to come to the aid of the *Star of the West*, which is also shown in detail in the insert. Fort Moultrie is to the left, the *Star of the West* is in the center, and Morris Island is to the right. (*Battles and Leaders of the Civil War.*)

**THE *STAR OF THE WEST*.** As the *Star of the West* steamed up the main shipping channel, Citadel cadets manning an artillery battery on Morris Island fired upon the ship. When artillery from Fort Moultrie joined the Citadel battery, the *Star of the West* turned about and returned to New York, failing in its mission to land troops and supplies at Fort Sumter. Some consider this action to be the first shots of the war. This image, published in *Frank Leslie's Illustrated Newspaper* on January 19, 1861, shows the smoke from the cadet guns off the stern of the ship, Fort Sumter off its bow, and the smoke from Fort Moultrie on the far right. (Fort Sumter National Monument Collections.)

MAJOR ANDERSON, LATE COMMANDANT OF FORT SUMTER CHARLESTON HARBOUR —SEE PRECEDING PAGE.

**MAJ. ROBERT ANDERSON AT FORT SUMTER, 1861.** A Kentucky native, he was a son of Col. Richard C. Anderson, who was among the patriots made prisoner of war at the surrender of Charleston in May 1780. Anderson was an 1825 West Point graduate and veteran of the Black Hawk, Second Seminole, and Mexican Wars. He was one of the army's most respected officers, and army commander-in-chief Gen. Winfield Scott selected him to assume command at Fort Moultrie in November 1861. (*Illustrated London News*, May 11, 1861. Fort Sumter National Monument Collections.)

SUMTER.

Capt. T. Seymour. ☆ ☆ 1st Lieut. G.W. Snyder. ☆ 1st Lt. J.C. Davis. ☆ 2d Lt. R.K. Meade. ☆ 1st Lt. T. Talbot.

☆ Capt. A. Doubleday. ☆ Maj. R. Anderson. ☆ Asst S. S.W. Crawford. ☆ Capt. J.G. Foster ☆

THE UNION OFFICERS AT FORT SUMTER IN APRIL 1861. Maj. Robert Anderson is seated second from the left. Capt. Abner Doubleday is seated at the far left. He commanded and aimed the gun that fired the first shot for the Union. After Sumter, he rose to the rank of major general of volunteers and saw action at Antietam, Fredericksburg, and Gettysburg. He is remembered as the originator of baseball, which he was not. Seated to Anderson's left are Assistant Surgeon Samuel W. Crawford and Capt. John G. Foster. Like Doubleday, Crawford became a general; he fought at Cedar Mountain, Antietam, Gettysburg, the Wilderness, and Petersburg and was brevetted for gallantry. Foster also became a major general of volunteers. He led a brigade in coastal operations in North Carolina. He ultimately succeeded Gen. Quincy A. Gillmore as commanding officer of the Department of the South and returned to Charleston in 1864 during the siege of Charleston. Standing are, from left to right, Capt. Truman Seymour, who became a major general of volunteers and commanded the unsuccessful charge at Battery Wagner in 1863; Lt. George W. Snyder, who died a brevet major on November 17, 1861, at age 28, after service in the First Battle of Bull Run; Lt. Jefferson C. Davis (no relation to the Confederate president), who fought at Pea Ridge and at Chickamauga and served as one of Gen. William T. Sherman's corps commanders; 2nd Lt. Richard K. Meade, a Virginian who, after his state seceded, resigned his commission, joined the Confederate army, and served through the Seven Days Battles, dying a brevet major on July 31, 1862, at age 26; and Lt. Theodore Talbot, who was promoted to major in August 1861 and who died on April 22, 1862. (*Harper's Weekly*, March 23, 1861. Fort Sumter National Monument Collections.)

**DEPARTURE OF WOMEN AND CHILDREN FROM FORT SUMTER, FEBRUARY 3, 1861.** The firing on the *Star of the West* convinced Maj. Robert Anderson and Gov. Francis Pickens that war was now a real possibility. Within a month, 42 women and children of the Fort Sumter garrison left the

fort aboard the steamship *Marion* for New York. (*Frank Leslie's Illustrated Newspaper*, February 23, 1861. Fort Sumter National Monument Collections.)

JEFFERSON FINIS DAVIS, PROVISIONAL PRESIDENT OF THE CONFEDERATE STATES OF AMERICA. Davis was a U.S. senator from Mississippi when his state seceded. Having graduated from West Point in 1828, he served in the U.S. Army until 1835. He settled in Mississippi, where he became a planter and was elected to the U.S. Congress in 1845. Davis resigned, became colonel of the 1st Regiment of Mississippi Riflemen, led them in the Mexican War, and was wounded. After the war, he served in the U.S. Senate from 1847 to 1851. He lost his bid for governor of Mississippi but was appointed Secretary of War from 1853 to 1857 by Pres. Franklin Pierce. He then returned to the Senate, serving until 1861. He believed he would be offered a high military command in the new Confederacy and, according to author William C. Davis, he was shocked and disappointed to be offered the presidency, which he reluctantly accepted. The situation in Charleston harbor became his first presidential problem. Because Davis ignored Robert B. Rhett in his selection of members of his cabinet, the *Charleston Mercury* took an immediate dislike to the president. Mary Chesnut wrote in her diary, "They believe SC is going to secede again"—this time from the new Confederacy. (Library of Congress.)

BRIG. GEN. PIERRE GUSTAVE TOUTANT BEAUREGARD. A Louisiana native, Beauregard grew up speaking French and probably did not learn to write and speak English until age 11, when he was sent to a private school in New York City. The school was administered by two Frenchmen who had served as officers in Napoleon's army. He attended the school for four years, and in addition to doing well in his studies, he was fascinated by his teachers' stories of their service with Napoleon. "Gust," as he was called by his family, began reading military history and decided upon the career of a soldier. He graduated second in the West Point class of 1838 and was assigned to the most prestigious branch of the U.S. Army, the Corps of Engineers. During the Mexican War the first lieutenant served on Gen. Winfield Scott's staff and earned brevet promotions to the rank of major. After the war, Beauregard returned to the peacetime duties of an engineer, but in 1858, he turned to politics and made an unsuccessful run for mayor of New Orleans. In November 1860, he was appointed as the superintendent of the U.S. Military Academy (West Point) to begin on January 1, 1861. He arrived on the 23rd and assumed his position; three days later, Louisiana seceded from the Union. A known secessionist, he was ordered to relinquish the superintendency. Beauregard complied on the 28th, earning the distinction of being West Point's superintendent for only six days, the shortest tenure in the school's history. Returning to New Orleans, he submitted a $165 receipt for mileage, which the U.S. government never paid. Beauregard then submitted his resignation from the army, which was officially accepted on February 20, 1861. Commissioned a brigadier general in the Confederate army on March 1, 1861, he was ordered to Charleston to assume command of operations in and around the harbor; he arrived in the Holy City two days later. (National Archives and Records Administration.)

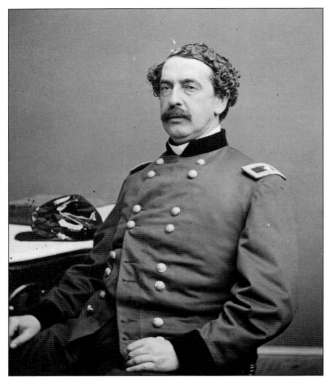

**ABNER DOUBLEDAY.** An 1842 West Point graduate, Doubleday was a native of New York. His grandfather had been a soldier in the Revolution, and his father served two terms in the U.S. Congress. Assigned to the artillery, he saw service in the Mexican War and by 1860 had risen to the rank of captain and commanded Company E, 1st U.S. Artillery Regiment. (Library of Congress.)

**SAMUEL WYLIE CRAWFORD.** A native of Pennsylvania, Crawford graduated from the University of Pennsylvania in 1846 then from the university's medical school four years later. In 1851, Dr. Crawford accepted a position as assistant surgeon in the U.S. Army. After service at several posts on the western frontier, he was ordered to Fort Moultrie in 1860. In 1887, his definitive history of the beginning of the war, *The Genesis of the Civil War, The Story of Sumter, 1860–1861,* was published. (Library of Congress.)

**ROSWELL S. RIPLEY.** Ripley was born in Ohio and graduated from West Point in 1843. He served with distinction in the Mexican War, receiving brevet promotion to captain. While stationed at Fort Moultrie, he married Alicia Middleton and resigned his commission. In 1860, he joined the South Carolina Militia. Commissioned a lieutenant colonel, he commanded the South Carolina Artillery Battalion and Fort Moultrie during the bombardment of Fort Sumter. When Southern forces moved into Sumter on the afternoon of April 14, 1861, Ripley became Fort Sumter's first Confederate commanding officer. Promoted to brigadier general in 1862, he served in the Army of Northern Virginia and was wounded in the battle of Sharpsburg (Antietam), Maryland. After recovering, he was given command of the First Military District, which included Charleston and Fort Sumter. The end of the war saw Ripley serving under Gen. Joseph E. Johnston in North Carolina. After the war, he moved to England, then to New York City, where he died in 1887. Ripley is buried in Magnolia Cemetery. (Library of Congress.)

HON. ROBERT BARNWELL RHETT, OF SOUTH CAROLINA.—PHOTOGRAPHED BY COOK, CHARLESTON, S. C.

ROBERT BARNWELL RHETT SR. South Carolina's leading and most well known secessionist, Rhett was born in Beaufort, South Carolina. He became an attorney in 1821 and established a thriving business. He entered politics in 1826 and at various times served in the state legislature, as state attorney general, and in the U.S. Congress and Senate until 1852. Rhett owned the *Charleston Mercury* and with his son Robert Barnwell Rhett Jr. as editor, the paper served as a platform to promote secession. In 1860, he played a major role in South Carolina's secession, was a delegate to the secession convention, signed the ordinance, and led the state's delegation to Montgomery, Alabama, to form the Confederate States of America. Rhett did not support the selection of Jefferson Davis as the Confederacy's provisional president and was not pleased when he was overlooked both for the Secretary of State and commissioner to England. He did not trust Davis and, after being slighted for the two posts he desired, he used the *Mercury* as a platform to criticize the president. The highest position the South Carolinian would hold during the war was as a member of the Confederate Congress. (*Battles and Leaders of the Civil War.*)

JAMES L. PETIGRU, SOUTH
CAROLINA'S PREEMINENT
LAWYER, WAS ONE OF THE
FEW UNIONISTS LEFT IN
CHARLESTON DURING THE
CIVIL WAR. Mary Chesnut
noted in her diary that
"Mr. Petigru alone in South
Carolina has not seceded."
Petigru famously said of
his rebellious state, "South
Carolina is too small for
a Republic and too large
for an insane asylum."
(South Carolina Historical
Society Collections.)

BRIG. GEN. PIERRE GUSTAVE TOUTANT
BEAUREGARD, THE HERO OF THE
BOMBARDMENT OF FORT SUMTER.
This portrait of the famous general
hangs in the council chambers of
Charleston City Hall. Note that
Beauregard is wearing a blue uniform,
not a gray one. Confederate gray
uniforms were not mandated until
1863. Beauregard was beloved in
Charleston, and as a reflection of
their feelings, the young men of the
city sent this telegram to President
Lincoln after the fall of Sumter:

> With mortar, cannon and petard
> We tender Old Abe our Beau-Regard.

(City of Charleston.)

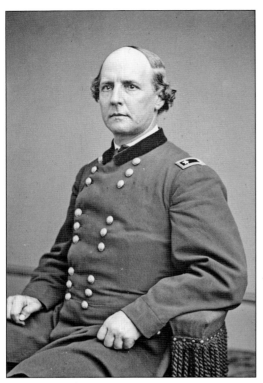

**Stephen A. Hurlbut.** Born in Charleston, Hurlbut lived in the Holy City for 30 years and became an attorney. In 1845, he moved to Illinois and entered politics. He served in the state legislature from 1859 to 1861, first as a Whig and then as a Republican. On March 21, 1861, President Lincoln sent Hurlbut and Ward Lamon to Charleston in order to ascertain the mood of the city. Hurlbut traveled with his wife and while in Charleston stayed with relatives. He met with James L. Petigru, businessmen, planters, merchants, and others and reported to Lincoln in part, "that there is no attachment to the Union" in Charleston. The Charlestonian was commissioned a brigadier general of U.S. Volunteers on June 14, 1861, and major general in 1862. (Library of Congress.)

**Maj. Robert Anderson in Dress Uniform.** Anderson's defense of Fort Sumter made him the Union's first national hero. Promoted to brigadier general on May 15, 1861, he was given command of the Department of Kentucky. However, the recurring effects of malaria and a severe wound, both from his service in the Mexican War, as well as the strain of field command forced him to relinquish his position in October. He was then assigned to command Fort Adams in Rhode Island. Anderson retired after more than 42 years of service, from a West Point cadet to a general, in October 1863. Though he was retired, Anderson was promoted to brevet major general of U.S. Volunteers. He returned to Fort Sumter on April 14, 1865, and in a formal ceremony with hundreds in attendance raised the same U.S. flag that had been lowered on April 14, 1861, when the fort surrendered. Anderson died on October 26, 1871, in Nice, France. His remains were returned to the United States and laid to rest in the West Point Cemetery. (Library of Congress.)

**WARD H. LAMON.** Lamon was a former law partner and trusted friend of Abraham Lincoln. On March 21, 1861, he and Stephen A. Hurlbut were sent to Charleston by the president to assess the situation in the city. There he met with James L. Petigru and Gov. Francis Pickens. The governor told Lamon, "Let your President attempt to reinforce Sumter, and the tocsin of war will be sounded from every hill-top and valley in the South." For reasons unknown, he erroneously told the governor that Fort Sumter would probably be evacuated. He also met with Maj. Robert Anderson at Fort Sumter, then returned to Washington and reported his observations to the president. (Library of Congress.)

1861 View of South Carolina Forces Building the Iron Battery at Cummings Point on Morris Island. The battery, which mounted three 8-inch Columbiads, earned its name because iron was placed on its exterior wall facing Fort Sumter. Edmund Ruffin was stationed here, serving as an honorary member of the Palmetto Guard, and he fired the first cannon from this fortification. The Point Battery and Trapier Battery were also located on Cummings Point and participated in the bombardment of Fort Sumter. (*Frank Leslie's Illustrated Newspaper*, March 30, 1861. Fort Sumter National Monument Collections.)

Confederates Preparing to Bombard Fort Sumter from Cummings Point. William Waud, an Englishman who had assisted in the construction of the Crystal Palace, made this sketch at Cummings Point on Morris Island as the Confederate army prepared to bombard Fort Sumter. It depicts a gang of slaves mounting a cannon. Waud worked for *Frank Leslie's Illustrated Newspaper*. His brother Alfred Waud was the most prolific of the Civil War combat artists. (Library of Congress.)

**FORT MOULTRIE HOT SHOT FURNACE.** Solid cast-iron cannonballs were placed inside the furnace until red hot. They were then fired at ships or buildings. Hot shot from the furnace in this photograph set fire to Fort Sumter's officers' quarters. The fire spread to the enlisted men's barracks and threatened the powder magazine. This ultimately lead to the surrender of the fort. Note the various implements used to move the hot shot and damage to the furnace from Union artillery fire from Fort Sumter. (South Carolina Historical Society Collections.)

**GUNS AT FORT MOULTRIE.** After South Carolina troops occupied Fort Moultrie, they constructed log and sandbag traverses to protect the guns used during the bombardment. The image shows some of the guns and members of the South Carolina Battalion of Artillery who fired on Fort Sumter. (South Carolina Historical Society Collections.)

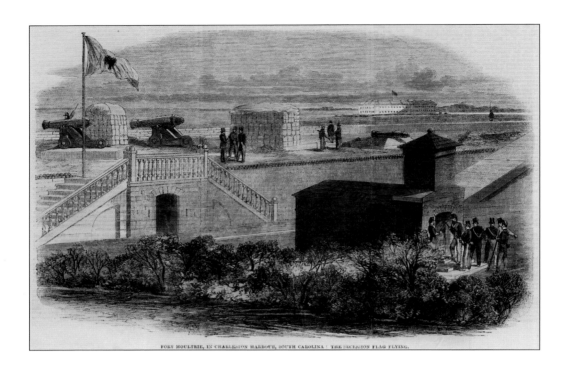

FORT MOULTRIE, IN CHARLESTON HARBOUR, SOUTH CAROLINA : THE SECESSION FLAG FLYING.

TWO 1861 VIEWS OF FORT MOULTRIE. After the Federals moved from Fort Moultrie to Fort Sumter, the South Carolina Militia moved into the Sullivan's Island fort and repaired the damages. The above image shows the hot shot furnace on the parade ground; above it and beyond the guns is Fort Sumter. The image below shows cannons along a section of the parapet. The above image appeared in the February 2, 1861, issue of *Frank Leslie's Illustrated Newspaper*, and the image below is from the January 26, 1861, issue of *Harper's Weekly*. (Both, Fort Sumter National Monument Collections.)

**THE FLOATING BATTERY.** This battery, positioned at the tip of Sullivan's Island, mounted two 32-pounder and two 42-pounder guns. Its construction was the idea of Confederate navy captain John Hamilton, and the South Carolina Executive Council gave him $12,000 to build it. The guns sat on an 80-foot-by-40-foot barge. At one end was timber framing covered with iron with embrasures (openings) for the guns to fire through, and attached to the rear was a small hospital. During the bombardment, the battery fired 470 rounds at Fort Sumter. (*Frank Leslie's Illustrated Newspaper*, March 30, 1861. Fort Sumter National Monument Collections.)

THE CHARLESTON HOTEL. Recognized as one of the city's best, it was located at Meeting and Hayne Streets. Radical secession delegates stayed here during the 1860 Democratic National Convention, and in 1861, the hotel was a popular location for public gatherings. This February 23, 1861, *Frank Leslie's Illustrated Newspaper* print shows Maj. Gen. Samuel McGowan, of the South Carolina Militia, addressing the Abbeville Volunteers from the balcony. (Fort Sumter National Monument Collection.)

**COL. JAMES CHESNUT JR.** James Chesnut had the distinction of giving the order that started the Civil War and of being married to Mary Boykin Chesnut, the author of the most renowned Civil War diary (*A Diary from Dixie*). Chesnut was an accomplished South Carolinian who had graduated with honors from the College of New Jersey (now Princeton University), studied law with James L. Petigru, and gone into practice in his native Camden, South Carolina. He served in state government and was U.S. senator from South Carolina when the secession movement was coming to fruition. He was the first U.S. senator to resign his seat. Chesnut was a delegate to the Montgomery Convention, which created the Confederacy, and was a strong supporter of Jefferson Davis for the presidency. (A fellow delegate resigned, saying, "Oh, I was tired of seeing Chesnut play rug dog to Jeff Davis.") He became an aide to Beauregard, and it was Chesnut on that early April morning who informed Major Anderson that General Beauregard "will open the fire of his batteries on Fort Sumter in one hour from this time." (South Carolina Historical Society Collections.)

**Capt. Gustavus V. Fox.** Gustavus V. Fox was the brother-in-law of Montgomery Blair, a member of a powerful Missouri political family and Lincoln's postmaster general. In early 1861, Fox argued forcibly to President Lincoln that Fort Sumter could be reprovisioned and reinforced. Fox came to Charleston in March to consult with Anderson and came back in command of the relief expedition in April. Later, as assistant secretary of the navy, Fox became obsessed with capturing Charleston. (Richard W. Hatcher III Collection.)

**FORT SUMTER.** In a December 9, 1860, report, Maj. Robert Anderson wrote from Fort Moultrie, "Fort Sumter is a tempting prize, the value of which is well known to the Charlestonians, and once in their possession, with it ammunition and armament and walls uninjured and garrisoned

properly, it would set our Navy at defiance, compel me to abandon this work, and give them the perfect command of this harbor." (*Harper's Weekly* supplement, April 26, 1876. Fort Sumter National Monument Collections.)

**FORT SUMTER, 1861.** This handsome painting hangs in the capitol in Washington, D.C. It is one of the three paintings of the fort by Brig. Gen. Seth Eastman, who painted the nation's principal fortifications between 1870 and 1875. Fort Sumter is the only one depicted more than once,

demonstrating its symbolic importance to the nation. Named for South Carolina's Revolutionary War hero Brig. Gen. Thomas Sumter, the fort was built on a man-made island in Charleston harbor. (Architect of the U.S. Capitol.)

FORT SUMTER'S SALLY PORT (MAIN GATE), AND A PORTION OF THE GORGE WALL, ESPLANADE, AND DOCK, 1861. It was through this sally port that Major Anderson and his command entered Fort Sumter on the night of December 26, 1860. First South Carolina and then Confederate representatives arrived here to meet with Anderson over the days and weeks before April 12, 1861. It was the exit through which Anderson and his men left on April 14, 1861, and through which the Confederate garrison entered the fort. The sally port was destroyed in the first major bombardment of Fort Sumter, beginning in August 1863. (*Frank Leslie's Illustrated Newspaper*, April 13, 1861. Fort Sumter National Monument Collections.)

**BOMBARDMENT FROM FORT JOHNSON, 1861.** The April 27, 1861, *Harper's Weekly* print is based on a Theodore Davis sketch. Engravers at the newspaper took his sketch and created this engraving of the bombardment from Fort Johnson. (Fort Sumter National Monument Collections.)

**THE APRIL 12–13, 1861, BOMBARDMENT OF FORT SUMTER.** This *c.* 1861 Currier and Ives print is one of many different views published of this historic event. (Library of Congress.)

**A View from Charleston of the Bombardment of Fort Sumter.** The view from the Battery looks up East Bay Street and reveals a military camp, stacked muskets, cannons, and soldiers and civilians alike watching the bombardment. Note the ladies with spyglasses on the upper piazzas of the first house. Jane Harbin wrote, "Early Saturday morning . . . I went down to the house of a friend on the battery and took my seat on the second story piazza. I saw every gun fired by friend and foe." The artillery on the Battery did not fire at Fort Sumter, and the fort did not fire on the city. (*Harper's Weekly*, May 18, 1861. Fort Sumter National Monument Collections.)

**Post–Civil War Book Plate.** This plate is from the title page of Joel T. Headley's 1866 book *The Great Rebellion; A History of the Civil War in the United States*. In this single image, the artist captures all the drama of the opening of the Civil War. South Carolina artillery, identified by the Palmetto flag, fire their guns as Fort Sumter burns, its flag flying in defiance. (Fort Sumter National Monument Collections.)

**ILLUSTRATION OF THE BOMBARDMENT OF FORT SUMTER.** This undated engraving represents one of innumerable images produced depicting the opening salvo of the war. (Fort Sumter National Monument Collections.)

**THE BLAKELY GUN AT CUMMINGS POINT.** The gun was singular in that it was the only rifled gun used in the bombardment of Fort Sumter. A British-made cannon, it fired a 12-pound solid iron projectile with amazing accuracy for the time period. A Charleston businessman living in Liverpool, England, Charles K. Prioleau, purchased the gun and shipped it to Charleston. He donated it to his native state to be used in its defense. General Beauregard wrote that it fired "with peculiar effect." (*Battles and Leaders of the Civil War.*)

HARPER'S WEEKLY.

A JOURNAL OF CIVILIZATION.

VOL. V.—No. 227.]     NEW YORK, SATURDAY, MAY 4, 1861.     [ SINGLE COPIES SIX CENTS. | $2.50 PER YEAR IN ADVANCE.

Entered according to Act of Congress, in the Year 1861, by Harper & Brothers, in the Clerk's Office of the District Court for the Southern District of New York.

THE HOUSE-TOPS IN CHARLESTON DURING THE BOMBARDMENT OF SUMTER.

**CHARLESTONIANS WATCH THE BOMBARDMENT OF FORT SUMTER IN THIS FAMOUS FRONT-PAGE ILLUSTRATION FROM HARPER'S WEEKLY.** A Charleston lady wrote a few days later, "Everybody crowded down to the battery, and stared with all their eyes at the forts and when Anderson's white flag appeared the shout was vigorous. We spent almost all of those two days down on the battery or in Mr. Louis DeSaussure's house at the corner [of East Bay and South Battery Streets] looking with the greatest eagerness for all that could be seen." (Robert N. Rosen Collection.)

**EDMUND RUFFIN, A VIRGINIA PLANTER, WRITER, FIERY SECESSIONIST, AND DEFENDER OF SLAVERY.** The author of *An Essay of Calcareous Manures*, he initiated an era of agricultural reform in the antebellum South restoring depleted farmland to productivity. Due to his age, fame, and the intensity of his devotion to Southern independence, Ruffin served as an honorary member of the Palmetto Guard, was stationed at the Iron Battery at Cummings Point on Morris Island, and was given the honor of firing one of the first shots of the war. (Library of Congress.)

FORT JOHNSON.      IRON-CLAD BATTERY, CUMMING'S POINT.      FORT SUMTER.      FORT MOULTRIE.

BURSTING OF THE SIGNAL-SHELL FROM FORT JOHNSON OVER FORT SUMTER.

**THE FIRST SHOT EXPLODES OVER FORT SUMTER.** At 4:30 a.m., April 12, 1861, a 10-inch mortar shell fired from the East Battery on James Island at Fort Johnson exploded over Fort Sumter, marking the beginning of the bombardment and the Civil War. This engraving presents a view of the first shot from behind the Iron-Clad (Iron) Battery on Cummings Point, Morris Island. (*Battles and Leaders of the Civil War.*)

**Capt. George S. James.** This pre–Civil War photograph shows James as a lieutenant in 4th U.S. Artillery Regiment. A South Carolinian, he resigned his commission when the state seceded, was commissioned a captain, and was given command of Company C, South Carolina Artillery Battalion. James and his men were stationed at Fort Johnson. Early on the morning of April 12, 1861, after Major Anderson rejected the final demand to evacuate Fort Sumter, Capt. Stephen Dill Lee and aide-de-camp James Chesnut "proceeded at once to Fort Johnson, which we reached at 4 a.m., and to Capt. George S. James . . . gave the order to open fire at the time indicated. His first shell was fired at 4.30 a.m." James was ultimately promoted to lieutenant colonel and commanded the 3rd South Carolina Infantry Battalion. On September 14, 1862, he was killed in the battle of South Mountain, Maryland. His body was never recovered. (Fort Sumter National Monument Collections.)

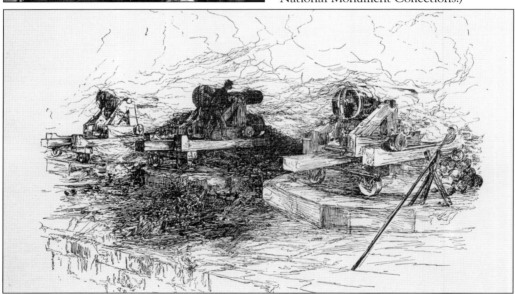

**Sgt. James Carmody.** Due to the heavy Confederate cannon fire, Major Anderson ordered his command to fire only the cannons in the first tier casemates. However, some of the fort's largest guns were on the barbette. These guns were already loaded and aimed. At one point during the bombardment, Sgt. John Carmody disobeyed the major's order, made his way to the top of fort, and fired the guns aimed at Fort Moultrie. "The contest," Sgt. James Chester said later, "was merely Carmody against the Confederate States and Carmody had to back down, not because he was beaten, but because he was unable, single-handed, to reload his guns." The drawing is by Theodore R. Davis after the event. (*Battles and Leaders of the Civil War.*)

**The Bombardment of Fort Sumter as Depicted in the Newspaper *Le Monde Illustré* of Paris.** Sumter is in the foreground; Sullivan's Island and Fort Moultrie are to the right. The town of Mount Pleasant is at the upper right, and Charleston is at upper left. The drawing is inaccurate as it includes a large nonexistent island in Charleston harbor. (South Caroliniana Library, University of South Carolina.)

SCENE ON THE FLOATING BATTERY IN CHARLESTON HARBOR, S. C. DURING THE BOMBARDMENT OF FORT SUMPTER.—From a Sketch by an Officer.—See Page 355.

**A VIEW FROM INSIDE THE FLOATING BATTERY.** This *Frank Leslie's Illustrated Newspaper* engraving depicts the battery in action during the bombardment. Although it was struck several times, it suffered no damage. (*Frank Leslie's Illustrated Newspaper*, April 27, 1861. Fort Sumter National Monument Collections.)

**ONE OF FORT SUMTER'S GUNS IN A FIRST TIER CASEMATE BEING FIRED.** The combination of firing guns and the fire in the fort's barracks and officers quarters on April 12 and 13, 1861, produced thick, noxious smoke, and this postwar engraving suggests a couple of ways the men protected themselves from the effects of the smoke. (Fort Sumter National Monument Collections.)

**GUNS IN ACTION AT FORT SUMTER.** From the first tier casemates, Union artillery returned fire on the batteries surrounding the fort. The thick smoke of cannon fire soon blended with the smoke from the burning buildings within the fort. (*Illustrated London News*, May 11, 1861. Fort Sumter National Monument Collections.)

**ACTION INSIDE FORT SUMTER DURING BOMBARDMENT.** This engraving from *Battles and Leaders of the Civil War* provides another view of action taking place inside Fort Sumter during the bombardment. (*Battles and Leaders of the Civil War.*)

**GUARD BOATS.** On the night of April 12, 1861, General Beauregard ordered guard boats to be positioned off Morris Island at the entrance to the main shipping channel. They were to be vigilant for any attempt by the U.S. Navy relief expedition to send reinforcements or supplies to Fort Sumter. The article accompanying this April 30, 1861, print from *Frank Leslie's Illustrated Newspaper* read in part, "The effect was picturesque and beautiful, as the boats rising and falling with the motion of the waves caused the flashing torches held by the men to dance in weird motion." (Fort Sumter National Monument Collections.)

**Guns in Action in Fort Sumter First Tier Casemate.** In this Currier and Ives print, Major Anderson stands to the left. It appears to be based on the May 11, 1861, *Illustrated London News* engraving. (Library of Congress.)

**Fire in the Enlisted Men's Barracks at Fort Sumter.** During the bombardment, Confederate mortar shells and hot shot set the barracks and officers quarters on fire several times. This April 30, 1861, *Frank Leslie's Illustrated Newspaper* engraving depicts one of those incidents. (Fort Sumter National Monument Collections.)

**Col. Louis T. Wigfall Arrives at Fort Sumter.** Early on the afternoon of April 13, 1861, the top section of Fort Sumter's flagpole was cut down by Confederate artillery fire, causing both it and the flag to fall to the parade ground. On Morris Island, Col. Louis T. Wigfall, one of General Beauregard's aides, seeing that the flag was down, assumed it to be the traditional signal for surrender and determined to go to the fort to inquire if Major Anderson wished to surrender or at least suspend the fighting. With the bombardment still in full force, Wigfall was taken in a small boat to the fort. The colonel arrived at Fort Sumter and made contact with a member of the garrison. Though Wigfall did not have the authority to negotiate a cease-fire or surrender, he did enter the fort and began an exchange with Anderson. Soon members of Beauregard's staff who did have the authority arrived, and a cease-fire and surrender were agreed upon. (From *The Civil War at Charleston*.)

**Peter Hart Raising the Stars and Stripes during the Bombardment.** At 1:00 p.m. on the afternoon of April 13, 1861, the top portion of the flagpole at Fort Sumter was cut down by cannon fire and fell to the parade ground. Members of the garrison immediately recovered the flag, still attached to the top portion of the pole. It was taken to the top of the fort's right face, where Peter Hart attached the flag to the wall. Hart had served as Maj. Robert Anderson's aide during the Mexican War, after which he left the army and became a New York City police officer. On January 6, 1861, Eliza Anderson, the major's wife, was allowed a brief visit with her husband at Fort Sumter. Hart had accompanied her from New York and was allowed to stay as Anderson's civilian aide at the fort. (Fort Sumter National Monument Collections.)

**INTERIOR OF FORT SUMTER AFTER THE BOMBARDMENT.** In the left foreground is one of the three 8-inch Columbiads placed on the parade ground as a mortar (though never used) to fire on Morris Island. The ruins are the burned-out officers' quarters, and in the center is the sally port (main gate). (South Carolina Historical Society Collections.)

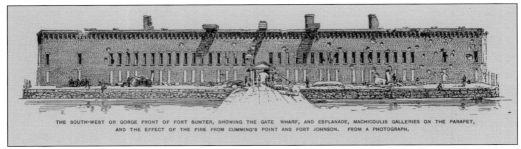

THE SOUTH-WEST OR GORGE FRONT OF FORT SUMTER, SHOWING THE GATE WHARF, AND ESPLANADE, MACHICOULIS GALLERIES ON THE PARAPET, AND THE EFFECT OF THE FIRE FROM CUMMING'S POINT AND FORT JOHNSON. FROM A PHOTOGRAPH.

PANORAMIC VIEW OF FORT SUMTER'S GORGE WALL. This view looks down the fort's dock showing the sally port (main gate), esplanade, and gorge wall. At various locations are the scars from Confederate cannonballs that struck the wall during the bombardment. (*Battles and Leaders of the Civil War.*)

PORTION OF RIGHT END OF FORT SUMTER'S GORGE WALL. Numerous points of impact from Confederate solid shot fired from Cummings Point on Morris Island are visible in this photograph. Notice the rubble removed from the fort's interior on the esplanade. (South Carolina Historical Society Collections.)

**FORT SUMTER'S FLAGPOLE.** At 1:00 p.m. on April 13, 1861, Confederate artillery fire cut the top section of the pole in half, causing it and the U.S. flag to tumble to the parade ground. Beyond the flagpole are the ruins of the officers' quarters. The fort's sally port (main gate) appears in the lower left. (Robert N. Rosen Collection.)

**TRAVERSE ON FORT SUMTER'S BARBETTE.** In the background of this photograph is the traverse at Fort Sumter's right shoulder angle, the corner where the right face and right flank wall meet. The traverse was constructed to protect the cannon mounted on the right flank parapet against artillery fire from Fort Moultrie. Traverses are used to protect a position from enfilading (flanking) fire. (South Carolina Historical Society Collections.)

**Ten-Inch Columbiad.** Major Anderson placed one of Fort Sumter's most powerful guns, a 10-inch Columbiad, on the parade ground positioned to fire like a mortar. It could fire a 128-pound solid iron cannonball or a 100-pound exploding shell, as well as other types of ammunition. Its purpose was to fire on Charleston, but it was not used. A group of South Carolina dignitaries who were touring the fort after its surrender stand around the gun. (South Carolina Historical Society Collections.)

**FORT SUMTER'S RIGHT FACE BARBETTE.** These guns face Fort Moultrie. The image reveals some of the damage suffered in this section of the fort. Charleston harbor is in the background. (South Carolina Historical Society Collections.)

**FORT SUMTER'S SALLY PORT.** After Confederate forces moved into the fort on April 14, 1861, they began repairing the damage from the bombardment. A pile of lumber has been placed in front of the sally port. Debris and rubble are evident on either side of the entrance. The gorge wall shows evidence of artillery damage. (South Carolina Historical Society Collections.)

**THE STEAMSHIP ISABEL.** Owned by the Moraccan Steamship Company, this ship transported Major Anderson's men from Fort Sumter to the awaiting federal fleet. M. C. Moraccai, who owned the company, was a state senator and prominent Jewish businessman in Charleston. (Charleston Renaissance Gallery.)

**INTERIOR OF FORT SUMTER.** The image was made shortly after the departure of Major Anderson and his garrison. The Confederate soldiers are posing for the slow-exposure camera. Note the First National Confederate Flag, commonly known as the "Stars and Bars." The photographer was either F. K. Houston or George S. Cook, both of whom were from Charleston. (U.S. Army Heritage and Education Center.)

**THE *LADY DAVIS*.** After the surrender and evacuation of Fort Sumter on April 14, 1861, Charlestonians crowded onto boats to visit the fort. One of these boats, the *Lady Davis*, arrives at the fort with passengers eager to tour the site of the battle they watched for two days. Note the First National Confederate Flag flying above the fort. (*Battles and Leaders of the Civil War.*)

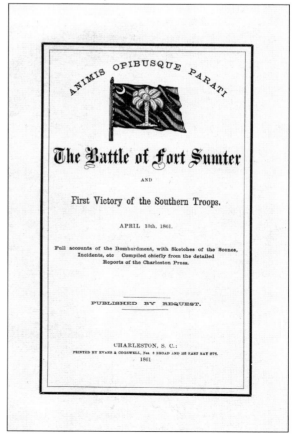

**THE BATTLE OF FORT SUMTER.** Evans & Cogswell of Charleston produced a 35-page booklet history of the bombardment of Fort Sumter within months of the event. They were offered for sale to the public. The Latin inscription at the top of the page, "Animus Opibusque Parati," is one of the mottoes of the State of South Carolina—"Prepared in Mind and Resources." (Richard W. Hatcher III Collection.)

**FORT SUMTER'S PARADE GROUND AFTER THE BOMBARDMENT.** Based on the numerous photographs taken of the fort after the bombardment, newspaper engravers created a variety of views for publication. The May 4, 1861, issue of *Frank Leslie's Illustrated Newspaper* provided its readers this view of the fort's interior. (Fort Sumter National Monument Collections.)

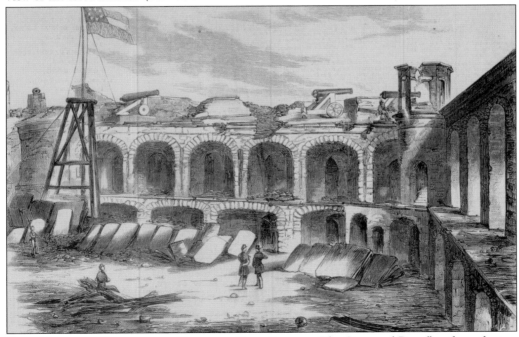

**FIRST NATIONAL CONFEDERATE FLAG OVER FORT SUMTER.** The Stars and Bars flew from the top of the hoist used to move heavy items, like cannons, up to the fort's third (top) tier. (*Frank Leslie's Illustrated Newspaper*, May 4, 1861. Fort Sumter National Monument Collections.)

**VIEW ACROSS FORT SUMTER TOWARD THE SALIENT ANGLE.** Seven Confederate soldiers pose on some of the thirteen 32-pounder guns lying on the parade ground. Behind them are two 8-inch Columbiads mounted as mortars to fire on Morris Island. (South Carolina Historical Society Collections.)

**REMOVING RUBBLE FROM PARADE GROUND OF FORT SUMTER.** In the days and weeks following the evacuation of Fort Sumter by the Federals, Confederates worked to remove rubble and repair damage to the fort. Two workers with wheelbarrows can be seen in the left foreground, while to the right, a group of officers and men look on near the base of Fort Sumter's flagpole. (South Carolina Historical Society Collections.)

**THE BARBETTE OF FORT SUMTER.** Shortly after Confederates moved into the fort on April 14, 1861, Charleston photographers arrived to take numerous images of the now famous fortification. This view shows three men posing for the camera during their examination of the guns along a section of the barbette. (South Carolina Historical Society Collections.)

**INTERIOR OF FORT SUMTER'S SALLY PORT.** Four of the men posing in the sally port are wearing military uniforms, though not all are identical. The man to the far left appears to be a civilian, although he is wearing a military kepi. (South Carolina Historical Society Collections.)

**VICTORIOUS CONFEDERATES.** A group of Confederate soldiers and a few civilians pose among the guns and rubble on Fort Sumter's gorge wall barbette. The remains of the roof of the burned-out officers' quarters appear on the right. (South Carolina Historical Society Collections.)

**A VIEW ACROSS THE PARADE GROUND FROM THE LEFT FACE OF FORT SUMTER.** This image reveals a much cleaner parade ground than what the Confederates found upon their entry into the fort on April 14, 1861. The 10-inch Columbiad in the left foreground was mounted in that location by the Federals. (South Carolina Historical Society Collections.)

**FRANK LESLIE'S ILLUSTRATED NEWS PAPER**

Entered according to the Act of Congress in the year 1861, by Frank Leslie, in the Clerk's Office of the District Court for the Southern District of New York.

No. 283—Vol. XL]     NEW YORK, SATURDAY, APRIL 27, 1861.     [Price 6 Cents.

## IMPORTANT NOTICE!

**To Officers and others Attached to the Armies of the Federal and the Confederate States**

I shall be happy to receive from Officers and others attached to either Army, sketches of important events and striking incidents which may occur during the impending struggle which seems to threaten the country. For such sketches, forwarded promptly, I will pay liberally.

My corps of Artists is unequalled in the country, and correspondents can depend upon their sketches, however rough, being produced in the finest style of art.

Any gentleman connected with either Army who will forward us a small sketch, as a specimen of his ability as a draughtsman, will receive, gratuitously, "Frank Leslie's Illustrated Newspaper," for the coming year.

Sketches of unusual interest will be most liberally paid for.

Special attention is requested to this notice.

FRANK LESLIE, 19 City Hall Square.

## The Only Reliable War Illustrations

The Illustrations of the Secession troubles in the South, in Frank Leslie's Illustrated Newspaper, are the only authentic and reliable sketches which have appeared. Four months since we dispatched a special Artist to Charleston, who has resided there ever since, visiting Columbia and Montgomery on occasions of importance, and furnishing us spirited and reliable sketches from all those points. During the past few weeks he has been on Morris Island, and was present there during the bombardment of Fort Sumpter.

Two weeks ago we despatched another special Artist to Charleston, who was present in that city during the whole of the fight.

Some of the results of our liberal enterprise will be found in the superb illustrations in our present issue. They are graphic and accurate, and are in advance of all other publications.

For several months we have had a special Artist stationed at Washington, who has kept our readers au courant with all the important events transpiring there.

It is by such enterprise that we distance all competitors, and sustain the proud position awarded us universally as the only Illustrated Newspaper in America.

The most convincing proof of the reliability and accuracy of our illustrations is, that ours is the only Illustrated Paper which is allowed to circulate freely in the South, and an additional proof is, that it stands a critical examination in those places where the scenes we illustrate occurred.

In the struggle which is fast approaching we shall retain our

REJOICINGS ON THE BATTERY AT CHARLESTON, S. C., DURING THE BOMBARDMENT OF FORT SUMPTER.—FROM A SKETCH BY OUR SPECIAL ARTIST.—SEE PAGE 355.

**CHARLESTONIANS CELEBRATING IN WHITE POINT GARDENS (THE BATTERY).** *Frank Leslie's Illustrated Newspaper* devoted half of the front page of its April 27 issue to the image of Charlestonians celebrating the bombardment of Fort Sumter. (Fort Sumter National Monument Collections.)

**CIVILIANS AND MILITARY WATCHING THE BOMBARDMENT OF FORT SUMTER.** No location offered a better view of the firing upon Fort Sumter than the open spaces of the Battery. Emma Holmes wrote in her diary: "The Battery was soon thronged with anxious hearts, and all day long they have continued, a dense, quiet, orderly mass, but not a sign of fear or anguish seen." (*Pictorial Battles of the Civil War.* Fort Sumter National Monument Collections.)

**EXCITEMENT IN FRONT OF THE MILLS HOUSE ON HEARING OF THE SURRENDER OF FORT SUMTER.** For 34 hours, civilians and military personnel in Charleston watched as Fort Sumter was bombarded. When Major Anderson surrendered on April 14, 1861, the city was jubilant. (*Pictorial Battles of the Civil War.* Fort Sumter National Monument Collections.)

**THE WASHINGTON LIGHT INFANTRY.** Composed of men from many of Charleston's best families, the Washington Light Infantry was posted on Sullivan's Island during the bombardment of Fort Sumter. It was one of numerous infantry units positioned at various locations around Charleston harbor to defend against any attempt by the United States to resupply or reinforce Fort Sumter. (Washington Light Infantry Collections.)

**CONFEDERATE LOOKOUT TOWER AT FORT WASHINGTON.** Members of the Washington Light Infantry pose for the camera near the lookout tower located at their fort on Sullivan's Island. They remained alert for any enemy boats that might attempt a landing on the island. (Washington Light Infantry Collections.)

**FORT MOULTRIE AFTER THE BOMBARDMENT.** Fort Moultrie had played a major role during the bombardment of Fort Sumter. Here a group of men stop to pose for the camera in the fort after the bombardment. (South Carolina Historical Society Collections.)

**A Battery in Fort Moultrie.** Members of the South Carolina Artillery Battalion pose for this photograph taken after the bombardment. Fort Moultrie's guns fired more than 700 rounds at Fort Sumter during the bombardment. (Fort Sumter National Monument Collections.)

**Effects of the Bombardment on Fort Moultrie.** The garrison at Fort Sumter concentrated most of its return fire on Fort Moultrie. Despite this, the fort received limited damage, some to the enlisted men's barracks. (South Carolina Historical Society Collections.)

**Monument at White Point Gardens to the Defenders of Fort Sumter.** Eight thousand Charlestonians attended the dedication of this monument on October 20, 1932, including the last Confederate veteran of Fort Sumter still living in Charleston. (Robert N. Rosen Collection.)

**PALMETTO FLAG RAISED ON FORT SUMTER.** On the afternoon of April 14, 1861, the Palmetto Guard was one of the Confederate units assigned to move into Fort Sumter after Maj. Robert Anderson's surrender. Pvt. John Styles Bird of the Palmetto Guard was the unit's color bearer. When he entered the fort, Bird made his way to the top of the left flank wall, which faced Charleston. There he placed the first Confederate flag raised on Fort Sumter. This photograph shows Bird with the flag at the national reunion of United Confederate Veterans held in Charleston in 1899. Today the flag is on display in the museum at Fort Sumter National Monument. (Fort Sumter National Monument Collections.)

**THE PALMETTO GUARD FLAG.** The flag held in the photograph of John Styles Bird is on display in the museum at Fort Sumter National Monument. (Fort Sumter National Monument Collections.)

**EDMONDSTON-ALSTON HOUSE.** The 1825 Edmondston-Alston House was used by Gen. P. G. T. Beauregard to watch the bombardment of Fort Sumter on April 12, 1861. Later that year, Gen. Robert E. Lee found refuge in the house during the Great Fire of 1861. The original family Civil War collections displayed in the Edmondston-Alston House Museum include an 1860 copy of South Carolina's Ordinance of Secession and the postwar pardon granted to Charles Alston and signed by Pres. Andrew Johnson. Like most South Carolina families, the Alstons lost a son to the war—1st Lt. John Julius Pringle Alston, 1st South Carolina Artillery, who died of typhoid fever after serving at Battery Wagner in the fall of 1863. (Middleton Place Foundation.)

# ABOUT THE TRUST

The Fort Sumter–Fort Moultrie Historical Trust was established to support the work of the National Park Service at Fort Sumter and Fort Moultrie National Monuments. Its board consists of local civic leaders, historians, and teachers. Park rangers serve as advisors. The trust raises money to support the forts and educational and historical programming about them.

The 150th anniversary of the Civil War, the sesquicentennial, presents a grand opportunity to study and commemorate the war. The trust has taken the lead in this commemoration by putting on seminars, programs, concerts, and other educational events on a variety of subjects such as secession, the causes of the war, the siege of Charleston, the Battle of Battery Wagner, the role of African Americans in the war, and the submarine H. L. Hunley. The story of the war will be told from Southern, Northern, and African American perspectives.

The trust is also raising funds to support local students, especially low-income students, to visit both Fort Sumter and Fort Moultrie and to provide programming about the Civil War in local schools.

# INDEX

# www.arcadiapublishing.com

Discover books about the town where you grew up, the cities where your friends and families live, the town where your parents met, or even that retirement spot you've been dreaming about. Our Web site provides history lovers with exclusive deals, advanced notification about new titles, e-mail alerts of author events, and much more.

**MADE IN THE USA**

Arcadia Publishing, the leading local history publisher in the United States, is committed to making history accessible and meaningful through publishing books that celebrate and preserve the heritage of America's people and places. Consistent with our mission to preserve history on a local level, this book was printed in South Carolina on American-made paper and manufactured entirely in the United States.

This book carries the accredited Forest Stewardship Council (FSC) label and is printed on 100 percent FSC-certified paper. Products carrying the FSC label are independently certified to assure consumers that they come from forests that are managed to meet the social, economic, and ecological needs of present and future generations.

**FSC**
**Mixed Sources**
Product group from well-managed forests and other controlled sources

Cert no. SW-COC-001530
www.fsc.org
© 1996 Forest Stewardship Council

Find Your Place in History.